PENNIES FROM HEAVEN

How To Get Them and What To Do With Them

by

Barrie Lawrence

Author of THERE MUST BE MORE TO LIFE THAN THIS
and THE CURIOUS CASE OF THE CONSTIPATED CAT.

Grosvenor House
Publishing Limited

All rights reserved
Copyright © Barrie Lawrence, 2018

The right of Barrie Lawrence to be identified as the author of this
work has been asserted in accordance with Section 78
of the Copyright, Designs and Patents Act 1988

The book cover picture is copyright to Derek Blois

This book is published by
Grosvenor House Publishing Ltd
Link House
140 The Broadway, Tolworth, Surrey, KT6 7HT.
www.grosvenorhousepublishing.co.uk

This book is sold subject to the conditions that it shall not, by way of
trade or otherwise, be lent, resold, hired out or otherwise circulated
without the author's or publisher's prior consent in any form of binding or
cover other than that in which it is published and
without a similar condition including this condition being imposed
on the subsequent purchaser.

A CIP record for this book
is available from the British Library

ISBN 978-1-78623-300-4

This book is dedicated to the members of the Norwich Full Gospel Businessmen's Fellowship (FGB), and to my fellow directors on the National Council of FGB UK&Ireland, for their love, support, encouragement and warm friendship, which is so greatly appreciated.

Other books by Barrie Lawrence

Christian

THERE MUST BE MORE TO LIFE THAN THIS!
New Wine Publishing (2012)

THE CURIOUS CASE OF THE CONSTIPATED CAT –
and other true stories of answered prayer
Grosvenor House Publishing (2016)

Light Autobiographical

A DENTIST'S STORY
Grosvenor House Publishing (2014)

PATIENTS FROM HEAVEN – and Other Places!
Grosvenor House Publishing (2015)

LICENSED TO DRILL – Dentist on the Loose!
Grosvenor House Publishing (2017)

'Prosperity is having all your needs met, and more. More - so you can give to the Lord, his people, and the poor'.

Don Double - Evangelist, and founder of Good News Crusade.

Contents

Prologue		xi
Introduction	Biblical Prosperity is For You!	xvii
PART ONE	PENNIES FROM HEAVEN. My Adventure	1
Chapter 1	Jesus First! (Austerity and a Lesson Learned)	3
Chapter 2	Rags to Riches	13
Chapter 3	Prophet and Loss	27
Chapter 4	Prophet and Gain	35
Chapter 5	Sonshine Out of Clouds	47
Chapter 6	Plundered	59
Chapter 7	Restored - and More!	65
PART TWO	PENNIES FROM HEAVEN. How to Get Them and What to Do with Them	75
Chapter 8	Pennies – How to Get Them!	77
Chapter 9	God's Purpose for You in Prosperity	85
Chapter 10	Pennies – What to Do with Them!	99
Chapter 11	Generosity	117
Chapter 12	Sowing and Reaping	127
Chapter 13	Wisdom	137
Chapter 14	Work	145
Chapter 15	Forgive Us Our Debts	153

Chapter 16	It Just Ain't Fair!	159
Chapter 17	True Love	165
Chapter 18	When It All Goes Wrong!	175
Chapter 19	When It All Goes Right!	189
Chapter 20	Be Happy!	199
Chapter 21	Promises, Promises!	203
	I Am Indebted…	211

Prologue

"You are a successful man", I was told by a number of people. Perhaps the white Lotus Esprit sports car identical to the one driven by 007 in the recent (at that time) James Bond film had caught their eye. Or maybe it was the fact that I had 5 dental surgeries with dentists and hygienists trying to cope with the thousands of patients - *my* patients - who flocked through the doors each day. And they no doubt had an opinion of how much my income might be. "You are a successful man", I was told.

But I was not. I was a *failure*. I was an *unsuccessful* man. I was someone who had got his life into a muddle, his relationships into a twist, and his emotions into freefall. I was stressed out of my mind. And that most certainly does not constitute success, even if one has a fast car, etc.

If the Bible is the inspired word of God (and of that, I'm totally convinced), then we are told, *"I pray that you may prosper in all things and be in health, just as your soul prospers"*, 3 John 2. But the priority is that the *soul* prospers.

Back in the garden of Eden, there was no problem. Adam and Eve had everything they needed, and more, to enjoy life on Earth. They had perfect fellowship with their Creator. He had created all things, and he was the source of all good things. And this state of blissful prosperity continued until the Fall.

Eve ate the forbidden fruit, and Adam quickly followed. Whether you take this story as literally true or not (and I am one who does), the message is clear - the human race is not where it was at the beginning. Things have changed, and the world is no longer the happy place we read about in the opening chapters of Genesis. Paradise lost was prosperity lost.

Man had cut himself off from his divine source, and there was no way back. We read elsewhere (Isaiah 59:2) that sin separates people from God, and that was graphically illustrated by Adam and Eve being expelled from the garden, and of cherubim being stationed at the entrance to prevent any return. Throughout the Old Testament we read of people separated from God, sometimes reaching out to him, and sometimes responding when he reached out to them. But for the most part, there is crime, violence, rebellion, wars, murders, idolatry and misery. And let us not blame God for what *man* has done.

Thank God for Jesus - and I certainly do. Jesus made all the difference, and continues to do so. Having lived a sinless life during which he enjoyed fellowship with the Father, he went to the cross, took our sin upon himself, and paid the price for it. Sin was gone, for those who chose to put their trust in him. They experienced the start of a new life. It was like being born all over again. Their spirit became alive as they came into fellowship with a loving Father, through the atoning sacrifice of Christ. And they started to prosper from the inside out.

Theology can be boring, but living in the truth of what the Bible teaches is a wonderful adventure. Because of Jesus, my whole life changed at the age of twenty-one back in 1965. It was the start of a new life, a different life, and a better life. It was not an easier life, but it was, above all, a fulfilled life. There were lessons to learn, and promises to enter into. My soul was prospering, and I knew joy that was a strength. I had lessons to learn, and though I was never in real need, there were times of testing. But God's word, the Bible, is the most trustworthy book (or library of books) on Earth. His promises are true, and his desire is for us to enjoy his fullness in all aspects of life.

Life was good. There was the excitement of realising the relevance of God's promises in a fallen, hostile world. I did not have all the answers, and still don't. But I know the One who does.

I prospered, by the grace of God. And then for a season, I compromised. We always have to take responsibility for sin, and compromise is indeed sin. I had many of the trappings of prosperity, but inside, my soul was far from prospering.

I was outwardly a *successful* man, but inwardly, and in reality, I was an *unsuccessful* man. Success and prosperity flow from the inside out. If you are a multi-billionaire with a glamorous wife (or wives), with a fabulous supercar (or supercars), and with a magnificent luxury palace (or palaces) with hundreds of servants, but do not have Biblical prosperity in your soul, you are a failure.

We were created for success. We were intended to be healthy. We were given the destiny of prosperity. So don't foul up your soul. Follow the teaching God gives us in the Bible, which I illustrate from my own life in this book, and prosper. Prosper the Biblical way, from the inside out.

Jesus, in the New Testament, applied the Old Testament Law as three principles. Firstly, put God first. So in practice, don't be obsessed with and focused on earthly things, or you will fall short of your destiny. Secondly, people are far more important than things. So in practice, truly love your neighbour and make that a priority, rather than chasing after *things*. If you make this mistake, you can again fall far short of your God given destiny. And thirdly, other people's needs are much more important than your rights. The *'Me! Me! Me!'* society is obsessed with *'my rights'*. Be aware of, and attend to, your neighbour's needs, and your Heavenly Father will reward *you*.

You see, I want to put material prosperity in context. The Lord made Abraham an extremely prosperous man, and he calls us children of Abraham (Galatians 3:29). Isaac, Jacob, and Esau, Abraham's son and grandsons, were all materially prosperous. I have quoted my friend Don Double, who defines Biblical prosperity as 'having your needs met, and more'. There may be a little more, a lot more, or somewhere in between, but that is the promise. There are other priorities, but the promise of 3 John 2 is still a promise!

I was unsuccessful, regardless of my car, my dental practice, my bank balance, etc. A short time later, the car had gone, there was very little bank balance, and I no longer had a wife - but I was successful on the inside. I had repented of my errors, and I had tried to put them right. If someone had prevented me, I had persisted in trying until I had peace in resting from such attempts. I felt I was now forgiving *their* unforgiveness, though I probably did not appreciate the hurt I had caused. And yet I *was* forgiven, and on the inside, my soul was prospering. And prosperity works from the inside out.

There have been traps and pitfalls set by our common enemy along the way. But taking two steps back has not prevented me from then taking three steps forward. Or, by the grace of God, ten steps. But I have had to get up when I have fallen, and it is the grace of God that enables us to do just that.

So get your soul right with God. Then *keep* your soul right with God. Follow the teaching we are given in Scripture - and prosper. *Prosper* in order to be a better kingdom-builder, because that is the primary reason why the Lord prospers his people. Be generous. Give. Help others. Shower kindnesses upon people. Love your neighbour more effectively. And use your prosperity to extend the Kingdom of God and glorify Jesus. Give - and he will give you yet more. That is the nature of our wonderful, generous Heavenly Father.

* * * * *

The Bible says: *'Beloved, I pray that you may prosper in all things and be in health, just as your soul prospers'. 3 John 2.*

Introduction

Biblical Prosperity is for You!

Have you ever wished for a financial miracle? I have. Or even prayed for one? That was me in 1973, 1974, 1983, 1984, 2002, and 2003. Those days were difficult and challenging, and I learnt many lessons. I want to share them with you.

Have you ever felt that you were perched on the edge of a financial abyss, and could slip off into dark despair and disaster any day? That was me in 1984 and 2002. More lessons learned.

Have you ever wondered how you were going to manage, with your income barely covering your basic needs and outgoings? I was there during the years 1963 to 1968.

Have you ever been on the mountaintop of 'no financial worries'? That just about describes my situation from 1975 to 1982, but I was probably unaware of how blessed I was, or of how my mishandling of it would lead to disaster. Another major lesson.

* * * * *

The heavy hand of the security guard at Tesco landed on my shoulder, bringing my exit to an abrupt halt. "Got you", he said, causing an immediate and intense flow of adrenaline that caused my heart to miss a beat, and then go into overdrive.

Suddenly, he was grinning. And then he started to laugh. "Remember me, don't you?" he said. He pushed up his peaked cap. "It's me. Ken. Surely you remember me. I went to the same church as you, Barrie".

Ah, Ken. It had been some years now. My memory was not what it used to be - or was it just too full, after many years of meeting people, doing things, visiting places, and so forth? But, I recalled dimly, Ken liked curry... Indian... and we had dined out a few times when his marriage had failed. It was starting to come back to me. What an amazing piece of kit the human brain is!

"And I still listen to the tapes of you preaching". And now he was grinning again. "Finance. *Money*. How to handle the stuff. My favourite tape of yours".

I had preached at that church quite regularly during my 25 years there. In fact, I was one of a small team who had preached often while our numbers increased from around 25, to 100... and then 200... and then 300 and more. Quite an act of God in a small Norfolk town of around 4,000 people. I had, no doubt, on occasions covered the subject of finance. Money. Dosh. Dough. We all need it, but how do we get it? And having got it, what do we do with it? The Bible has a lot to say about it. Money and possessions are mentioned over 800 times according to *Forbes.com* – a company that deals with money, investment, business, etc. 800 times? – I guess the Lord is telling us that it is important, and that we need to understand the subject.

"My favourite tape", Ken repeated. "Love 'em. Really helpful. Honestly".

I would have been hard pressed to tell you what was on those tapes. But it seemed that the one thing Ken was saying to me was that I knew something of what the Bible taught about money. And I always illustrated my teaching with examples from my own life. Why did he still play them? Some people might think that was rather sad, but I guess it was because he felt he was hearing God speak to him through them. Through me even.

* * * * *

I may not recall what I taught during those heady days when our church was growing so fast, but I will always remember the excitement, and sense of the presence of God amongst us. No other church in the area was outgrowing buildings in the way ours was, and people seemed to come to faith in Christ almost weekly. And then, having bought a building, growth stabilised to some extent. We employed a pastor, like 'normal' churches did, and those of us who had preached and taught during the growth phase were deemed largely redundant in that respect.

There were occasions when a member of the old guard *was* asked to preach on a Sunday morning, and on one occasion I was asked to speak specifically on 'Money'. Then it was mentioned to me that a local barrister from another denomination would be visiting us that morning, and I almost died. Money - how boring was that? What would the learnéd gentleman think of our humble congregation? "Come, Holy Spirit, and inject divine life into my preach", I begged. I can only vaguely remember that morning and the preach, but a week or two after that, I heard that the illustrious man had visited, and had decided to *join* our church. Now, perhaps twenty-five years later at the time of writing (2018), he himself has a congregation of several hundred (Oh yes – he went on to leave the law and entered the ministry full time) where *he* is the preacher. No doubt he sometimes teaches on the subject of 'Finance'.

But it was many years earlier when I found that I had to really study the Bible with regard to the subject of finance. I was asked to, as the church I was part of needed money. And needed it badly. Let me tell you about it.

* * * * *

A church was meeting in our home in the early 70's. Over a period of approximately two years, we grew rapidly from around eight to about seventy people, many of them in their teens and twenties. Together with two other men, I was deemed to be an elder. Well, I was relatively senior - I was twenty-nine! With so many of our congregation sitting shoulder to shoulder across the floor, we jokingly said that when one got up, they all got up, because they were stuck together in the sweaty heat. It was uncomfortably tight in our sitting room (especially for those on the floor), and so we moved to a community centre, where it was decided that someone should go into pastoral work full-time. An elder was chosen, but there were insufficient funds. Although we had little in the way of overheads (house churches should not really have much in the way of overheads), there was a surprisingly small amount in the collection each week. The answer, apparently, was for me to teach on the subject of 'giving'. I searched the Scriptures with regard to the theme, 'Finance in the Bible', reading and studying what both the Old and New Testaments had to say on the subject, and then delivering a weekly series of four forty-five minute teaching sessions. After my first session - wonder of wonders - the collection doubled. It was still insufficient to support a full-time worker, but an encouraging increase. After session two, it doubled again. Amazingly, the amount given doubled after each of the four finance sessions. "Go on Barrie - give us a fifth one", said the elder-cum-aspiring pastor. But I had exhausted all that I had learned from my studies, and so the series ended. The nominated elder left his secular employment, and worked for a number of years in the church.

Clearly, my teaching on financial giving helped propel our church into the league where there were paid ministers. But a number of years later I was again asked to speak in some depth on the 'M' word when I was part of a church that already had a paid minister, but wanted a paid building. So let me now tell you about that.

* * * * *

It was around twenty years after the house church days that I found myself in a Wesleyan church. Ken was a member. It grew fast.

We felt we lacked integrity in remaining part of the Wesleyan denomination, as we were baptizing believers instead of infants, the baptismal font was being used as a birdbath in an elder's back garden, the pews had been removed and made into pigpens for a local school that presumably included farming in their curriculum, and the harmonium had been replaced with guitars, saxophone and drums. We became an independent evangelical church. However, there was a problem, in that we kept outgrowing the buildings we were renting, having made an exodus from our own little chapel a couple of years earlier. So our church launched out to buy a bus station. The vendors were asking £175,000, and we had just £2,000 in our church bank account. The final cost, with renovation and refurbishing would be £435,000.

In faith, we signed the contract to buy the building. We started a 'Bank of Jesus' - people loaned money, but withdrew when they liked. Some later converted money from a loan to a gift. My function was as director of finance – 'treasurer' in most churches. I taught on finance, exhorted the congregation, attempted to motivate, and oversaw all matters financial. Some people gave jewelry. Most gave money. Some cashed in savings policies. The combination of a generous people and an amazing God saw the project completed with no borrowing from the banks or any other organisations. Not a penny. And along the way, the Lord opened up the Scriptures, and taught me so much more about finance.

* * * * *

In this book, I want to tell you some of my own story, which is an adventure of lessons and miracles. I want to share with you some of the Biblical fundamentals I have learned with regard to receiving money, as well as principles concerning what we are expected to do with it. Whenever I teach or preach, I try and illustrate from my own life and experience, which gives me two problems with regard to writing this book.

Firstly, I have written autobiographically in other books; not about money and finance, and often in a rather light-hearted manner. Indeed, if you are amused by stories of people losing their false teeth down toilets and out of bus windows, or of a patient fleeing from my dental surgery and being chased through a country town by yours truly, then you might like to read my previous volumes. In this tome, though, I am concerned with the very serious matter of finance. Yet there is inevitably some overlap with my previous writings. I have written before, perhaps, of how I was led to buy a certain dental practice, or of the pain and heartbreak of divorce; in this book I consider the financial aspects of these, and other, situations we might encounter. Where there is a degree of duplication, I apologise. It has to be.

Secondly, there is a scripture that tells us that, with regard to giving, our left hand should not know what our right hand is doing (Matthew 6:3). The meaning is quite clear, in that we should not be giving, and then publicizing in order to win the praise of people. But I feel that writing from my own life and experience is generally the most helpful way of illustrating the Biblical truths that I wish to share. And so, forgive me if you feel I am wrong, but where I deem it to be useful, that is what I have done. I do not think you will praise me too much, as there is perhaps somewhat limited material to draw from in this area. Bear in mind too, that there is a cost to me in that I might be losing something of my heavenly reward (Matthew 6:1). Furthermore, and again in order to be helpful, I try to share something of my failings, as that might also enable you, the reader, to identify with me.

* * * * *

I trust that I have learnt the lessons, and I can tell you with enthusiasm that I have enjoyed the miracles. But most of all, I have learnt that life is all about Jesus, who is our *supply*.

Read on, and may you too learn the lessons and enjoy the miracles, and know that what the Lord has done for me, he can most certainly do for you.

* * * * *

The Bible says: *'And God is able to make all grace abound toward you, that you, having all sufficiency in all things, may have an abundance for every good work'. 2 Corinthians 9:8.*

PENNIES FROM HEAVEN
PART ONE
* * *

My Adventure

Chapter 1
Jesus First!
(Austerity - and a Lesson Learned)

"Let's talk about money", said my fiancée, as we sat together on the bed in my small room in the students' hostel in the East End of London. The bed? - well, there was only *one* chair. So we sat together and talked, and we had questions we could not answer.

The following Sunday, in church, we heard our pastor say, "This evening, I am going to talk about money". Well, how amazing was that!

* * * * *

Viewing the white Lotus parked at a rakish angle outside my city dental practice, patients might have thought that I was born with a silver toothbrush in my mouth. But that was far from the truth.

My father was a bank clerk, on a modest salary. My mother was a housewife. Unpaid. But my childhood was generally a happy one. The day started with a cooked breakfast, usually bacon and eggs (my parents kept chickens), and after school, there was a cooked supper. I bicycled miles every week, exploring the Norfolk countryside, and bringing home frogs, leeches, lizards, coypu carcasses... which in a rather circuitous way, led to my career in dentistry (read my earlier books).

At an early age, I had been severely traumatised by a dentist. In my mid-teens, I decided that I could do better. Maybe I could be a *kind* dentist. Even, a gentle dentist. Were dentists paid well? I had no idea. I never thought that way, but just wanted to look after peoples' teeth, and not hurt them. I was not a star academically, but I studied all hours of the day, and many of the night. I discovered that I needed to go to a dental school, at a university - and so I read all about dental schools and universities. (No-one in our family had ever been to a university - they were posh schools for delinquent young adults, weren't they?). I applied, and was accepted at the London Hospital, in Whitechapel. That is in the East End of London, as well as being the cheapest property on the Monopoly board. My parents were proud of me.

Until I went to university, finance was not something I ever thought about. Why should I? – I lived at home with my parents, and had little spare time, being either at school or studying at home for the education certificates necessary to enter dental school. My father gave me a few shillings a week for pocket money, though I hardly had time to get out and spend it. But university meant I was away from home, and having to think for the first time about income and expenditure. My government grant just about sustained me, with around £8 a week coming in and around £8 a week going out. I lived in a University hall of residence, and when I was thrown out for bad behaviour, was taken into the students hostel at the hospital. And it was there that the whole direction of my life changed dramatically. Forever. No looking back.

I was an atheist. I was taught at school that humans had developed from monkeys, which had themselves developed from more primitive creatures, and so on, right back to when living cells first appeared. Where did *they* come from? - we were not told. I'm not sure whether we were taught that everything came from nothing through a 'big bang', though I was mindlessly swallowing all that I was taught at that time. I was just a Norfolk boy, and the teachers were masters in black gowns. Awesome - they knew almost everything. I went to a church, and observed ancient grey-haired pensioners with hearing-aids being told they should be kind, and that the Bible was not really true, and there would be a jumble sale on Saturday... That clinched it – the God I had read about in the Bible was nothing like that. He did not exist. Clearly.

And then in my first week at University, there was a social gathering for new students. I was with a group of chaps, and most of us were drinking beer, and bragging, as young men do. Then one of the group said quite casually (and I forget the context), "But Jesus Christ has changed my life". What! I had thought he was intelligent. He was training to be a doctor? How crazy was that - he needed to see one. Badly.

It was still my first year at dental school, and I met a girl at a dance, and asked her out on a date. Then she told me that Jesus Christ had changed *her* life. So that relationship didn't go very far, or for very long. Goodbye.

It was nearly two years later that the intensity of lectures, clinics, exams, and student parties almost brought me to a breakdown. The doctor prescribed *Librium* to calm me down, and shortly afterwards I again bumped into that early girlfriend. She told me I needed Jesus. In fact, it seemed that almost everyone I met at that time told me the same thing. Whitechapel was crawling with Christians. I seemed unable to avoid them.

At this point, I will let you into a secret - actually, God was reaching out to me. He sovereignly directs all of history, and when you keep meeting Christians, it's because he has planned it.

It caused me to debate with Christians, read the Bible, and offer up occasional prayers, such as, "*Are* you there?" And one day, whilst in my study, I became aware of his presence, and about a month later, I knelt down in that same room and surrendered my life to Jesus. I changed in many ways, but I summarise what happened by saying that a very unfulfilled atheist became a very fulfilled child of God.

* * * * *

I may have changed, but my finances did not. These were days of austerity for me. Students with wealthy parents were supported largely by them, and usually drove sports cars. However, the majority of us did not come from families with that sort of money, and were given a grant by the government. £8 a week may not sound much today, though it was worth more in the 1960's of course. But to be frank, it did not sound very much then either! In my final year (1968) the grant had increased to £12 a week. It was the bare minimum I needed to live on, but in my first year or two, I had still managed to buy beer and cigarettes. It was a strange phenomenon I had observed in others, that those with virtually no money could always buy beer and cigarettes, so it seemed!

Jesus changed me, though I still drank beer (but not so often) and also enjoyed wine. The wine cost little, as I consumed it at the University Wine and Food Society, where it was greatly subsidised. In fact, I won the London University Sherry Essay competition in 1964, and was second in the University Wine Tasting competition the same year. So I was certainly learning something at University!

My values were changing, and I was coming to realise that my Creator had brought me into this new life, not just to bless me with joy and fulfilment, but also to serve him. He was more than a Saviour; He was Lord. Lord of everything. Lord of my money? But my main concern was that I was really living on the edge, with hardly a penny to spare.

* * * * *

And so I found myself sitting on my bed with my fiancée. "Let's talk about money", she said. I'm not sure whether we talked about her finances, as they did not seem to be a problem to her. But I felt that mine were. Could I cut back on my expenditure? It did not seem to be possible, as the hostel was a cheap place to live, with breakfast and dinner included. Lunch was inexpensive, joining my fellow students in the college refectory. Transport costs were minimal, as I walked to the dental school on site. Clothes? They never wore out, it seemed. Could I increase my income? I was in lectures and clinics all day, and studying most of my evenings and weekends. Unlike other University students, I had officially four weeks holiday a year. So there was not much scope for earning additional money.

The following Sunday, in church, we heard our pastor say, "This evening, I am going to talk about money". Wow – that just had to be God.

How could I get more? How could I spend less, even? But as far as I recall, his sermon was about money being a 'neutral' commodity which we can use for good or for evil. We have to be responsible in the way we use it. Well, I had precious little to use, and had little opportunity to use it for good or evil. I used it to exist. Then it was all gone.

But there was one thing I came away with that evening; Jesus is Lord, and we should put him first in all things, including money. And that constituted quite a challenge for me.

* * * * *

Our knowledge and understanding of kingdom matters increase as we regularly spend time with the Lord, reading the Scriptures, listening to those with a teaching ministry, etc. My understanding that Jesus should come first in a Christian's life was not based on a thorough knowledge of the Scriptures, but - I knew that Jesus should come first.

'Seek first the kingdom of God', (Matthew 6:33). That was a familiar scripture that tells us to put the Lord first. It may not explicitly say that we should give money to the Lord and his kingdom before budgeting for other needs, but that concept is implicitly there. I was reading Scripture regularly, thinking about it, and meditating on it, and I felt challenged to take practical steps to put Jesus first with regard to my finances. However, every penny was accounted for, which made the task seem impossible. Or was it? Had I not read somewhere that nothing is impossible with our God?

I suppose I had been vaguely familiar with the Ten Commandments from an early age. In middle class England at that time, there was a feeling that keeping those commandments was what decent people did. But I was coming to understand that the Lord did not want us to live a life of simply ticking divinely ordained boxes, but to fulfil the essence of the Law - to put him first, to honour him, and to please him. The opening verses of Exodus 20 spoke of having no other gods before the Lord. He was first.

I was also familiar with the twenty-third psalm. Everybody was in those days, and a significant number of people could recite it, whether they were active Christians or not. The Lord was my shepherd, and therefore, I would not lack anything I needed. I started to realise that this meant that I could trust him to look after *every* need. Even finance.

I was not so familiar with the promise of Philippians 4:19, but when I did read it, I realised that it sat very comfortably with the rest of the teaching that I was imbibing from the Bible. 'God would supply all my need according to his riches in glory in Christ Jesus'. Even before I came to believe, I suspected that there was infinite wisdom in the pages of Scripture. Now I was coming to love my Bible, as the Holy Spirit spoke to me through verse after verse, and book after book.

But how in practice could I put Jesus first with my rather meagre finances? From where would the money come? Would I really keep body and soul together?

* * * * *

It is so easy for us to 'talk the talk'. It costs us nothing to say "Jesus is Lord", but am I doing it? Do I 'walk the walk' as well as 'talk the talk'? I want to help my readers, as indeed others have helped me. But I have also been challenged at times, and that has caused me to grow. So, I want to challenge you, the reader.

The challenge for me was this - and I suggest you consider it too. Forget the 'talk' that says "Jesus is Lord", and consider the 'walk'. That means that what we actually *do* is so much more important than what we say. There are two things we have and which we can spend. We can spend them how we like but - we can spend them only *once*. These two commodities are so important. One is time, and the other is money. Spend them how you like. Your decision. But you can spend them only once.

I was challenged, because I was saying, "Jesus is Lord", but my time and money were being used largely the same way they were before I became a Christian. Also, they were being used in much the same way decent unbelievers used them. I needed to 'walk the walk'. We are called to be *different*.

So much of my 'free' time, when I was not in lectures or clinics, was taken up with study. I have mentioned that I am not an academic star, and passed exams by putting in hours of study. There was no photographic memory for me, and no honours degree. Basically, most evenings I had dinner in the hostel, and then studied from 7 p.m. through to 2 a.m.. I needed that time, though I usually made a few coffees whilst studying, and sometimes my fiancée would call round for coffee with me.

I made a decision with regard to giving time to Jesus. This decision was that to give practical priority to Him with my time, I would spend 30 minutes, from midnight to half past midnight, in Bible study and prayer. Bible study helped me get to know *about* the Lord, and prayer helped me get to know Him. That time was virtually sacrosanct, and with my door locked, lest intruders tried to invade for hospitality and coffee, I enjoyed time with Jesus, 'walking the walk'.

But how about my money? "Jesus is Lord", I vocalised. But did it change my walk? I wanted it to, but every penny seemed accounted for. Have you been there? So how, in practice, could I 'walk the walk'?

Nothing is impossible with our God. He makes a way where there is no way. I prayed, and considered. I thoughtfully prayed, and prayerfully considered. And the way opened! I had a good cooked breakfast provided at the hostel, and a dinner in the evening. Did I really *need* lunch? I made changes to my routine. Sometimes I would take a round of toast to my room after breakfast, and later, when my colleagues went to the refectory for lunch, I would retire to my room. Occasionally I would have nothing to eat. Sometimes I would have toast. Sometimes I would buy an egg, boil it in a kettle, and use the water for coffee. This released the cash I had previously spent on lunch. I obtained a missionary box and put 10 shillings in it each week. That was in 'old money', which was decimalised in February 1971. 10 shillings became 50p, and that in 1966 would be worth around £8 at the time of writing. Not a fortune, but to a dental student living in austerity, 'walking the walk' at last.

In fact, it was no great hardship. I was being more consistent in my faith. The Lord is no man's debtor, and I did not feel I was going without anything I needed. It was a foundation that I have tried, by the grace of God, to build on, 'walking the walk'. And I want you to know this - it's fun! Jesus said it is more blessed to give than to receive (Acts 20:35), which means that there is more fulfilment, joy, and feel-good factor in giving. In fact, I felt I was being set free. *Fun!*

How about you? I'm sure you are 'talking the talk', but are you really 'walking the walk'? Time and money - are you walking the walk? Remember my situation at dental school, where I had no spare time and no spare money. How about you? Is anything too hard for the Lord?

* * * * *

The Bible says: *'Seek first the kingdom of God and His righteousness, and all these things shall be added to you. Therefore do not worry about tomorrow'. Matthew 6:33,34.*

Chapter 2

Rags to riches

"We advertise that we *always* back dentists wanting to buy practices, but - you're the exception. The practice you are looking at is a dead duck. Don't touch it", said the representative of a finance company specialising in dentists.

He did not know the amazing power of God towards his children, even in the world of business.

* * * * *

Rags? An exaggeration of course, but I was not living in the style of other dentists. I was unaware, however, that I was shortly to experience the blessing of God in a way that would not only surprise me greatly, but also change my life dramatically. It also brought new challenges.

I sometimes say to fellow Christians that we don't always know 'what is around the corner' in life. However, we do know '*Who* is around the corner'. Sometimes he is there to protect, or comfort, or strengthen, or provide. And sometimes he is there to simply bless us.

My university days were multi-educational. I learned not only to examine, scale, drill, fill, crown, extract, and replace teeth, but also to distinguish a burgundy from a claret, and a Sauvignon Blanc from a Chardonnay. Spanish Reds were to be avoided at all costs in those days, whereas Hungarian *Bulls*

Blood and German *Black Tower* and *Blue Nun* were cool. Though we did not say 'cool' in the 1960's. Those who indulged in these beverages were 'with-it'.

I was also learning much about the real meaning of life. Because our Creator could not be seen, touched, handled, etc. I had previously assumed that he did not exist. Britain was well into becoming secularised, and I had been unknowingly saturated in the process. Radio, television, cinema, newspapers, magazines, and increasingly in education, life from the smallest virus to the largest mammal, plus the rest of the Universe, was explained in purely secular terms. The Big Bang theory was starting to gain ground, and left little room for the Creator God we read of in the Bible. Now, for me, all this was changing as my eyes were being opened to a dimension that is hidden from so many. My world view was coming into line with what I was reading in the Bible. What a book, or really, collection of books! I had always assumed that wisdom was to be found within its pages, but the amazing internal evidence that self-authenticates it as the inspired word of God was blowing me away. I was learning about the nature of the Creator, who was now my Heavenly Father. There were promises for me, and also responsibilities. One promise was that he would always look after me, and one responsibility was that I should put him first in all aspects of my life.

I have related how I wanted to walk the walk with regards to having Jesus as Lord in my life, and of the challenge that presented when it came to money. I had no spare cash, as every penny seemed to be needed to keep body and soul together, and yet in going without lunch, I was rarely hungry, and always had more than sufficient on my plate at breakfast and dinner.

I also found that there was sometimes enough cash left over at the end of the week to enable me to take my fiancée to a Chinese, or even better, an Indian restaurant. I can remember my first ever visit to an Indian restaurant some years earlier, and as an unbeliever, thought I had discovered heaven on earth. Later, I would see how hot I could take the curry, and my fiancée would count the prawns or assess the chicken to estimate the amount of protein that was on our plates. That was important in those days, apparently. Maybe the time would come when I would be able to visit an Indian restaurant *every* week. In fact, around twenty years later, in 1984, I would be visiting an Indian restaurant *twice* every week. Bliss - prosperity indeed!

Then there was the generosity of Morry and Sylvia, my fiancée's landlord and his wife. I would sometimes use their local corner shop for provisions, and they became my friends. They would tell me stories about the Kray twins, who were becoming famous for charity boxing matches, and infamous for murdering people. Morry and Sylvia's respective families had known them since they were children. "Strangling cats ain't natural", said Sylvia's elderly mother. "They never was normal. Normal people don't strangle cats, they don't". Whitechapel was, at that time, predominately Jewish, and there was a great sense of 'owning' the hospital which dominated the area. "You poor students, working all hours, and looking after our teeth", was a commonly held sentiment.

"Sylvia and I have been talking, and we have decided that you are going to have lunch with us every Tuesday. No discussion, cos we've decided. Be here at one o'clock, cos that's when you're getting it", Morry told me over the counter one day. There was to be no payment, because I was a poor student. I was to ring their front door bell, and the *au pair* would let me in. And so it was, every Tuesday, week after week and month after month, I was shown into the dining room by Consuelo, the Spanish *au pair*, who would serve me soup, followed by steak (always steak), and a pudding, followed by coffee. Morry and Sylvia were always too busy working in the shop, which was open 365 days a year (except leap years). I would occasionally be asked to accompany Morry on an evening drive around London clubs where he refilled his cigarette machines. I had to guard the cases of cigarettes while his back was turned. One of the clubs had a hole in the ceiling where Ronnie Kray had pulled out a Luger and fired it to 'make a statement'. In fact, I had missed one of his murders by just twenty minutes a year or two earlier. (See *A Dentist's Story*).

Chinese meals. Indian meals. A three course steak lunch every Tuesday. Together with my general feeling of well-being from the indwelling Holy Spirit, life was better than I had ever known it. And I was putting around a tenth of my meagre income into a missionary box, and praying it would contribute to others experiencing something of the life I was now enjoying, as they too came into relationship with their Heavenly Father.

Importantly, I did not give with any thought to receiving. I had not come under the 'plant a seed, and expect to reap a reward' type of teaching, and had not really seen a connection between giving and receiving. I gave because I wanted to put Jesus first in all things, including money. I wanted him to be Lord. I wanted to walk the walk. I just wanted to give to God.

* * * * *

I qualified in December 1968, and celebrated by taking my fiancée to the most prestigious Indian restaurant in London. Then I went home for Christmas, before driving down to Dorset in my rusty, agéd Hillman Minx.

Why Dorset? Until a few months previously, I had assumed that I would go into practice in Exeter, because my fiancée's family owned property there, including dental surgeries. Then, I was informed that there was a problem, and the door closed. With my qualification fast approaching, I needed to find a position in a dental practice. And quickly.

Many of my colleagues had very clear ideas concerning where they wanted to work. More importantly, they knew what car they wanted, and what lady they wanted in the passenger seat. Fast - both! There were practices that promised an above-average income which would enable them to enjoy their chosen lifestyle, and such opportunities were an obvious attraction.

Me? I wanted to continue to walk that walk, but was not sure how to go about it. So I prayed. Surely there was a heavenly plan for my life - but how could I find it? The obvious choice of location had been closed, so what other doors might open. The next obvious step was to look through the classified ads in the *British Dental Journal*, and then perhaps to find an agency. Whilst considering this, a letter arrived from a man I had met whilst working on a beach mission the previous summer, informing me that he knew of a young Christian dentist working in Dorset, who was almost unable to cope with the volume of work in his practice. The sender added that he did not know anything about my situation, such as where I was with my studies, but felt that he should let me know about the Dorset situation.

It is difficult to describe quite how I felt when I read that letter. 'My soul was flooded with excitement, anticipation and assurance' is perhaps too poetic, and maybe to say I felt like jumping up and down would be more realistic. I obtained the telephone number of Reg Carnall, and informed him that the Lord was sending me to help. He was not convinced, and understandably wanted an interview. Which resulted in me catching a train down to Dorset, and spending a few hours with Reg in Shaftesbury. He asked me questions, and showed me the practice. Also the town of Shaftesbury – quaint, picturesque, and totally delightful. We agreed that the way forward was clear.

I moved down to Dorset, lodged in a farmhouse just out of town, and commenced gainful employment in my chosen profession. Well, fairly gainful. Too much work for one dentist to handle is not necessarily enough work for two dentists. In general practice, most dentists are paid by the amount of work they carry out, which presupposes that the work is walking in through their surgery door. I kept an account of my weekly earnings, and in my first week, I earned £7. That was £5 less than my student's grant had been a month earlier, but it was worth more in those days, of course. And it slowly increased, though I was quite unconcerned, as I went for walks admiring the splendid views from that ancient Saxon hilltop town during the quiet periods. I would read my Bible, and started learning some New Testament Greek. Reg, the practice owner, was more concerned about my lack of work than I was, and after a couple of years, persuaded me to work part-time elsewhere to supplement my income.

There were expenses to be met. Initially I was living in a room on a local farm, where breakfast and supper were provided for me. I was getting married in a few months, and would then need to rent a property. My rust bucket of a car was an inconvenience at times. Twice the handbrake came off in my hand due to the rust, and on two occasions half the gears stopped working, again due to corrosion. There was no *MOT* testing for vehicles in those days, or I would have been off the road in no time. Eventually I traded it in for a somewhat younger car, with the sum of £5 being the trade-in value of my Hillman.

I married, and we were more than contented. During my five happy years in Shaftesbury, I never had a car that was new, or even nearly new. No problem. We bought a new dining room table and chairs, and bedroom furniture, but the lounge suite was secondhand (or fourth-hand or fifth hand) and smelled strongly of smoke. My wife made covers for it, having made patterns from old newspapers. Not what most young dentists and their families expected, but more than adequate. Again, no problem. Our first two daughters were born. We went to a local church, but I was increasingly preaching around the area, and also starting to become involved with evangelistic tent crusades.

* * * * *

"I have been feeling for a while that it is time to move", I said to my wife in early 1973. We both wanted to be real about such matters, having Jesus as Lord of my work. Where did *He* want us to go? We looked at one or two practices around fifty to one hundred miles away, and then heard of a practice for sale in Norwich, in my home county of Norfolk, much further away. There was the same feeling as when I had received the letter telling me of the Shaftesbury practice in late 1968. We prayed, of course. And then there was a vision. A man in a church we were visiting had a picture of a knight. Not a gentleman in shining armour, but a chess piece. He thought it was for my wife and I. Later, we looked at a map, and if a knight were placed on Shaftesbury, one of the places it could move to would be Norwich. This was not exactly conclusive, but together with our feelings after viewing the practice, and despite it being run down, with little treatment being carried out on the few patients attending, and its poor state of repair, we felt convinced that it was the Lord's direction for us.

I handed in my notice, which despite the background excitement at the new chapter of life opening up, was a sad occasion. Reg and his wife Eunice were good friends to us, and we would never forget those five wonderful years. I negotiated a price for the Norwich practice, comprising two dilapidated terrace houses, ancient equipment (some of it, including extraction forceps, rusty), and goodwill. There were finance companies who specialised in dentists, and one stated in its advertisements that it *always* backed dentists. Until I approached them.

"We advertise that we *always* back dentists wanting to buy practices, but - you're the exception. The practice you are looking at is a dead duck. Don't touch it", said the representative of the finance company. So how could I raise the necessary cash?

My father had worked in a bank, and one of his former colleagues was a manager. He arranged to meet him for lunch, and after the man had consumed a few beers and returned to work, I went in to ask him for a loan. Maybe I exaggerate, especially about the beers, but he entertained my request for a loan to enable me to buy the practice.

"And the monthly repayments will enable you to repay the money over ten years", said my new friend.

However, I found this rather alarming. The practice was costing more than a house; in fact, more than two houses. And for a house, one was generally allowed twenty-five years. Just ten years to repay such a large sum? Did he not know it was a 'dead duck' that did not generate much income? Had he not noticed this when he looked through the practice accounts? Could he not see that people did not come to this practice? Well, not many people.

"Ten years seems a short period of time to repay so much money", I said, and explained, "There are not so many patients attending the practice, and the dentist selling it to me only makes £2,000 a year. Before tax, if he pays tax on such a small income. My wife and I hope that more people will come to the practice, but I will need several times the number of patients he is seeing, and that could take a few years to build up. Perhaps I could repay over twenty-five years?"

But this was a business loan, and would have to be repaid in ten years. I thanked God (and the manager) for the money now being available, but also prayed, "Help Lord! If this is really where you want me, please work a miracle".

* * * * *

"Give them toothache, Lord, and cause them to come to *me*!" was *not* what my wife and I prayed. But we did pray. We prayed that the Lord would bring people in, and that I would be able to help them. We prayed that I would be able to stop the pain, when that was the problem. We prayed that people would want me to treat other dental problems that they had. We prayed that I would be able to point people to Jesus through being kind, and simply telling them of my experience of the living God.

The building was dilapidated, and needed repair and redecoration. The equipment really needed replacing in its entirety. The waiting room had a collection of old chairs, with no two alike. They would need replacing. The office was a tip. There were a few derelict rooms upstairs. One was full of magazines and dental journals, piled high, and obviously thrown in at random. It would seem that the door would be opened, a magazine thrown in, and the door shut quickly before they started sliding out. Another room was full of plaster models of teeth, which had been used for the construction of crowns and dentures. There were piles of them, and they too appeared to have been lobbed in to simply dispose of them. There was so much to do. We decided that redecorating the waiting room would be as much as we could manage with what little money was left after buying the practice.

A few days before I officially opened, I bought wallpaper and adhesive, and started giving the room a smarter appearance. There was so much papering to do, I was working alone, and it took so long. I was tired out, and worked at it until well past midnight for two days.

I walked into the practice the next morning, and stood there admiring my work. Until I found that I had placed three of the sheets of wallpaper upside down. One could tell because the flowers in the pattern were growing upwards in most of the room, but downwards in three sections! I really had been too tired. So much for the smarter, professional appearance. And so there was more work that would take more hours, removing upside-down wallpaper, and rehanging new sheets. By the time I opened, at least the waiting room walls looked half-decent.

I had advertised for a receptionist, and just one lady applied. She had done nothing like it before, but seemed pleasant, was the only applicant, and so had a successful interview.

I advertised for a dental nurse, and the extremely pregnant wife of an airman on a local RAF base, applied. She had some experience, and could work for a couple of months. My family and I were living temporarily with my parents, around twelve miles from the practice, and the airbase was *en route*. So for two months, I had time to advertise again, and take on a girl who could be trained.

But would there be enough work for me to make a living, and repay the loan? My wife and I assumed that if we were right in believing that this was the practice the Lord had directed us to, then everything else would be taken care of. We prayed. And we prayed.

* * * * *

I arrived at the practice for my first day's work there, and a few patients who had been attending regularly for years, were booked in to have their teeth checked. There were some emergency toothaches, and other people phoned to arrange to have their teeth examined. There were certainly more patients than my predecessor had ever seen. Would there be enough to enable me to keep up repayments on the loan? And then came the phone call that changed everything.

"Welcome to Norwich, old boy. Good to have you here. Just wondering if you could do us a favour? Well, you might be able to help a bit. We have a rather unusual situation in the city just now. Three dentists have retired, and couldn't sell their practices. So they have closed them. Just simply *closed* them. The end. Trouble is, old boy, they have sold their premises for development, and thousands and thousands of patients now have no dentist. I'm secretary of the Local Dental Committee, and it's my job to find them a practice. Impossible, of course. *Impossible*, old boy. So, any chance you could see just a few of them. Every little helps. Just asking".

Could I help? You bet I could. Did I have space in my appointment book for more patients. Yes - for thousands! And so I thanked him for his call, and said, "Just send them along".

It seemed like a stampede. The phone was continually ringing. The front door was opening, closing, opening, closing. There was a queue at reception. I suddenly found out how to work a lot faster than I had ever done before. And my wife and I were praising the Lord for leading us, and providing for us.

The loan that I envisaged struggling to repay over ten years, was paid off in ten months. *Literally* ten months. Gone. Finished.

We had bought a fairly modest house in the city. It was adequate for our family at that time (a third daughter had joined us), and most of the ground floor was just one room. Around a dozen people had joined us there to worship on Sunday mornings. And Sunday evenings. And midweek. We now found that we could invite people to stay for lunch on a Sunday, and our dining room table usually found at least a dozen people seated round it. Then the church grew to around seventy, which was uncomfortable with the majority sitting on the floor, shoulder to shoulder. But they were young! We soon moved the church into a community centre not far away, but still had people in and out of our house seven days a week.

However, after two or three years, and with the family growing, it was no problem purchasing a five-bedroomed, handsome double-fronted house in a more salubrious area of the city.

I had arrived in Norfolk with my pregnant wife and two daughters, driving an agéd, high-mileage Hillman Hunter estate car, bought from the local vicar, and still reeking of his dog. Now, my elderly vehicle was traded in for a new Volvo estate car. Brand new! I had never really dreamed of owning a *new* car. We could now transport our family, and people from the church, in relative comfort.

My appointment book was full to capacity, but the amount of money now flowing in, and the empty rooms upstairs in the practice, enabled me to expand. Very soon there was a second surgery, with a newly qualified young Christian dentist welcoming an ever increasing stream of patients. The following year a third surgery, with another newly qualified young Christian dentist joining us. After a pause of two years, I added two more surgeries, with another dentist and a hygienist, and a manned education unit where we could teach children how to brush their teeth properly, and help the local community to enjoy better dental health. The latter was funded by the practice; in other words, it made a loss. Likewise spending one day each week visiting housebound people, and treating them in their homes. I bought a portable dental unit, and even crowned people's teeth while they sat by the fire in their favourite armchair. The National Health Service was not interested in covering the cost of this service, but the Lord enabled me to do so. With other dentists working back at the practice, and a cash flow to support such work, I could spend one day a week helping those disadvantaged by poor health, low income, and often, advanced years. The work of the church was growing too, and so I could work in the practice three or four days a week, whilst using the other time to help people pastorally.

What an amazing God. He had changed my life back at university, and taught me how to put Jesus first. That had included the area of finance, and yet I had never been in serious need. In fact, giving to the Lord money that I could not afford, had led to even greater fulfilment in life. He had led me to Dorset, to a situation where I was earning so much less than most other dentists. But I had time to become familiar with the Bible, to take opportunities to preach and teach, and to help with evangelistic tent crusades. I was learning that fulfilment did not come from having wealth, but from enjoying a relationship with my Heavenly Father, through Jesus.

I had not really started with rags, and I had not become a millionaire. But having walked faithfully, by the grace of God, with Jesus for several years on a modest income, I had found that he was all I needed. Now he was showing me something different - riches. However, my fulfilment still came from my relationship with him. That, I had learned.

And yet, there were challenges to be faced. Challenges that wealth brings. Challenges that I found myself unable to handle at times. And if we do not learn things the easy way, then a loving Heavenly Father will teach us some other way. Even, the hard way.

I was totally unsuspecting, but extremely difficult days lay ahead for me.

* * * * *

The Bible says: *'The blessing of the LORD makes a person rich, and he adds no sorrow with it'. Proverbs 10:22.*

Chapter 3

Prophet and Loss

"You're going to lose everything. *Everything*", said Rod. He was clearly upset and spoke with a sense of urgency. "I don't see myself as a prophet, but I woke up with a scripture; several verses. And it is for *you*. This just doesn't happen to me - *words* like this. I'm really worried for you".

A few months later I had lost almost everything.

* * * * *

The Lord had prospered me since coming to Norwich. Arriving in the city around eight years previously, driving a rather ancient car and with next to nothing in my bank account, I had bought a practice which had been labelled 'a dead duck' by potential financial backers. In fact, they had backed off. And then God had stepped in, and I had been amazed at how rapidly the Lord had prospered me. A ten year loan had been paid off in ten months, entirely by the profit produced by the 'dead duck'. I had proceeded to add a second surgery at the end of my first year - then a third, and a fourth, and a fifth, plus a dental health education unit, a dental hygienist, and so on.

The ancient car had been replaced with a brand new Volvo estate to help transport my growing family in greater safety and greater style. Then I bought a Jaguar, and after that, a Lotus for me and a sensible estate car for my wife. The years of financial austerity were largely forgotten, as I now faced the challenges of prosperity.

It's interesting how people see us - and evaluate us. A rather sullen young man walked into my surgery, and remarked, "Wish I was a dentist", and proceeded to verbally drool over the Lotus parked outside the practice. He saw me as successful. He saw me as someone who had made it. But he looked on the outward appearance, oblivious that all was not well on the inside.

I adopted a somewhat defensive posture, and explained that he *could* become a dentist. "You can do it", I told him. "I managed it. You need five Ordinary Level GCEs including English and maths, and three Advanced Level GCEs including biology or zoology, and then five years studying at a University dental school. For no pay, and working all day and studying all evening. I did it. You can do it, and then you too will be a dentist". He scowled and laid back and opened his mouth. I quietly sympathised with him, because I was privileged. But I was also blessed by God, and my answer had perhaps betrayed something of pride. I was starting to attribute my success to my hard work, and hours of study. Of being unpaid whilst those who left school at the same time as me were out working and earning money. Of me being rewarded. But do we ever deserve wealth, money, riches? Should we not be working because we are called by God to do so, and whilst enjoying our relationship with him, thanking him for all the good things that we receive?

It's so easy to evaluate others, and ourselves, by 'what we have got.' And also to evaluate ourselves by 'rewards for what we have done'. But the Lord looks upon the heart.

* * * * *

I had known Rod for a few years. In fact, during that time, our respective families had been friendly, and for a while, had gone to the same church. We had enjoyed a day together on a boat on the Norfolk broads, and Rod's family were a local legend in their own time for showing hospitality. We certainly enjoyed their hospitality on many occasions.

But Rod was no longer the smiling, good-humoured companion I had known as my friend for the past few years. He was deeply concerned. More than that, he was alarmed. Maybe I had hinted that all was not well, but...

* * * * *

The Lord Jesus had been so good to me. My whole life had been changed, and what I had been experiencing was nothing less than a taste of eternity. That's what you get when you seriously turn to him - joy, health, fulfilment, every need met, and an overflow of divine blessing. I had promised to follow him all the days of my life - and yet...

And yet, I had compromised. My heart was to follow Jesus. Always. And yet... material prosperity had presented more challenges and temptations than I had ever experienced during the days of austerity. I had never known what it was to have money to the extent that it had flowed in during my early years in Norwich. A one surgery practice had become a five surgery practice, and dentists, hygienists, nurses, receptionists, and thousands of patients were providing me with an income that was previously beyond my wildest dreams. I no longer had to consider whether I could afford things. If I wanted something, I could have it. And that new facility led to a new attitude to life in general, and had resulted in me experiencing inner turmoil and chaos.

I still loved the Lord who had done so much for me, but I had let down so many people. And they were people I loved, and who loved me; my family who depended on me, and Christians who looked to me as an example. The Lord had shown this to Rod in a dramatic manner.

I don't think Rod would ever have seen himself as a prophet, and yet he was a prophet to me. In the Bible, prophets brought God's word to God's people. Usually. And occasionally, they were sent to people who would not be seen as 'God's people', such as Jonah going to Nineveh in Assyria. Rod was sent to me.

"Read Proverbs 5 for yourself", said my friend with his eyes staring, and his face white as a sheet. "I woke up, and knew I had to read this passage. It's dreadful. You're going to lose everything. Everything".

I knew Proverbs 5, because I had read the Bible from cover to cover so many times. And before that, I had read through it slowly, prayed, meditated, and made notes on every chapter. *Every* chapter. I may not have been a naïve young man as depicted in this chapter, and I may not have 'done what he did', but the principle was clear. There is a saying, 'If the cap fits, wear it' – and the cap fitted. The passage may not have been one hundred per cent accurate when it came to detail, but it was close enough.

I spoke about my situation with another friend. He was a man who had been something of a spiritual father to my wife and I for many years. He was a full-time evangelist, and he did not beat about the bush. He looked me in the eye and said, "Repent, or you'll go to hell". For those with a theological frame of mind, and of a Calvinistic persuasion, that might present a problem. But it was sobering, and I feel that at times we pussy-foot around too softly when it comes to the issue of sin.

The Lord was not pleased with me. People may think that God does not exist, or, that he does not mind too much if we stray a little at times, or, that he will never intervene when we slide away from the one we have committed to follow and serve.

But he does know, and he does intervene - and he does so in ways that cannot fail to grab our attention. Also, he warns us, through Scripture and through prophets and prophetic words. Like Rod. Like my evangelist friend.

But here is a conundrum. There are times when we know we are wrong, God speaks powerfully to tell us he knows and is displeased with us, and although we want to get our life straightened out, we seem unable to do so. That was my situation.

Now, don't misunderstand me. We are always responsible for our own decisions, behaviour, conduct, etc. But there are times when it is as though we have foolishly stepped onto the top of a slippery slope, and then found that though we desperately want to get off, we are sliding increasingly faster downwards. We may feel unable to forsake the wrong way, and follow the right way, but - we are always responsible for those decisions. Maybe only those who have been there can really understand.

At such a time, there is a chaotic whirlpool of unhelpful emotions which are so difficult to handle correctly, and in a manner that resolves the problems. When I told my wife what a mess I was in, the mistakes I had made, the wrong decisions that had brought me there, and so on, she tried to understand and help. But with both parties hurting, and a breakdown of trust, it was difficult to move forward together. I think she wanted to forgive. I think she wanted the marriage to continue. But in the same way that I had felt unable to change, *she* now found difficulty. I will not elaborate, except to say that what I experienced in my life at that time, and what I believe my wife was experiencing, helped me to handle a future situation in a godly manner. The oft-quoted Scripture, Romans 8:28, tells us that the Lord will bring good out of *everything* for those who truly love God. Lots of bad things were happening to me at this time, but they were lessons to learn, and the Lord used them for good in the days to come.

Rod was to me, a prophet. And the loss that he envisaged was soon to become a reality. My wife and I separated. I was offered a home with Christian friends, and took it. I naïvely assumed that there would be forgiveness and reconciliation, and perhaps a better future than could ever have been imagined before. One does read such stories. I lived with this lovely Christian family for six months, and they were so kind and supportive. They covenanted with two other couples, to pray daily for the restoration of my marriage - or for clear indication that it would not be restored.

As many of my readers will appreciate, the financial implications are huge. The family I stayed with never charged me a penny for my board and lodging with them, which was a tremendous blessing at such a time. However, there was significant increased expenditure in ensuring that my wife and four daughters were more than adequately covered financially, in order to reduce as far as possible any further anxiety during what must have been an emotionally traumatic time for them. It costs far less for six people to live under one roof, than for five to live there and one somewhere else. The Lord was good to me in so many ways, and not least in sustaining my health and strength. Another expense was engaging a solicitor to try and effect a reconciliation with my wife. He also advised making the separation 'judicial', which maximised the amount of money my wife received by reducing the tax paid. He was a Christian, and it was reassuring to know that one more person was praying for me at such a time. But solicitors are expensive. Even more than dentists!

It was some months later that three Christian friends brought me advice. They did not know each other, and yet within the space of a week or so, each suggested that continuing to seek reconciliation could make me seriously ill. I felt that this was godly wisdom, but not what I wanted to hear. I set a deadline of six months from having moved in with the Christian family. I reached the deadline, and reconciliation seemed as far away as the Moon. I moved into a small cottage, learned to cook, launder and iron, and started out on a whole new life. As a single man.

There were times when almost overwhelming sadness would seem to descend on me, but I occupied myself with decorating my new home, keeping chickens and ducks, and generally spending time doing what King David did during the difficult times – I encouraged myself in the Lord.

If separation carried huge financial implications, then starting life again in a new home only increased those commitments. In effect, I was paying two mortgages, two home insurances, and a lot more besides. My country cottage was tiny, yet delightful. But my home, wife, savings, reputation, etc. had gone. Rod had indeed been a prophet to me.

And so for the next *twenty years*, I supported my wife and children, bumping along on the overdraft line, but being looked after by my Heavenly Father. He had taught me things. He had brought me to repentance. I had tried to put things right with people here on Earth – yet had been prevented.

But now the Lord really stepped in and started blessing me in ways that made others feel, 'That's not fair'. Exactly - God's not fair. It's called grace. It's called mercy. It's called forgiveness. It's called restoration. It's not fair – but that is the nature of our Heavenly Father to those who seek him in sincerity. Read all about it in the next chapter!

* * * * *

The Bible says: *'The LORD sees not as man sees; for man looks on the outward appearance, but the LORD looks on the heart'. 1 Samuel 16:7.*

Chapter 4

Prophet and Gain

"You are proposing to open a new practice?" said my accountant. He was clearly feeling troubled by my announcement. "There's a fifty-fifty chance you won't make it, you know. Especially in your present situation". I opened the practice, and held my breath.

* * * * *

There are times when the Lord leads one to do things which are against all logic and reason. Joshua was told to march his army in silence round the enemy city of Jericho once a day for six days, and seven times on the seventh day. And then to blow a trumpet and shout. That was not the logical way to attack a fortified city, and yet... Read Joshua 6.

Elijah challenged the prophets of the heathen god Baal, making two altars on the summit of Mount Carmel. There had been no rain for three years, and the wood on the altars would have been as dry as tinder. The God who answered by fire would prove himself to be the true God. The prophets of Baal prayed, shouted, and pleaded, but there was no fire. Elijah dug a trench and filled it with water, and threw more over the sacrifice on the altar. If the dry altar of Baal had not caught fire, then drenching the Lord's altar with water was not logical. And yet... Read 1 Kings 18.

Goliath was a seasoned soldier, a man of war, and a giant in armour. David was a lad, with no sword, no armour, and no experience of war. To run towards Goliath armed with a sling and five stones was not logical. And yet... Read 1 Samuel 17.

There are some common features to the three well-known stories I have alluded to above. In each, we have a man of God who seeks to serve the Lord, please him, and obey him.

In each we have the people of God experiencing or having recently experienced, the Lord's discipline because of their disobedience. Joshua led a people whose parents had turned back from entering the promised land that they were told to enter. Elijah was a prophet to the people of God, who were largely apostate in following the heathen religion of Baal worship. David had arrived at the battlefield where the Israelite army fled to their tents whenever Goliath appeared. These were hardly examples of a nation with a living faith in God.

And yet each story is an example of the Lord's people being forgiven, *and* being restored. The rebellion in the wilderness, and refusal to enter the promised land, was behind the people of God as they approached Jericho. They were now to enter the land in victory.

Elijah's great step of faith on Mount Carmel was a huge leap forward for Israel. Baal was judged. Baal's prophets were destroyed. Ahab and Jezebel's days were numbered. The drought was over. The people of God could move forward again.

Until David arrived on the scene, the Israelite army had fled every time Goliath stepped out and challenged them. We read that David ran forward. He killed Goliath, and Israel advanced, regaining lost land right up to the gates of the Philistine cities.

Our God is a God of compassion, forgiveness, empowerment and restoration. We read accounts demonstrating this countless times in the Bible, and he is the same today. Have you experienced failure? Have you 'fallen from grace'? Do you find yourself in a position of financial need? Then read the Bible, and understand that our God is a God of mercy, compassion, forgiveness, victory, success, abundance, and prosperity. He does not change. What he's done for Joshua, Elijah, David and Israel, he will do for *you*.

In 1983 I saw myself as a failure. I had let my God down. Also, my wife, my family and my church. My fine handsome double-fronted 5 bedroomed house was gone, and my car would soon follow. I had little cash left in the bank, and was dependent on the kindness of a Christian family who took me in and did not charge me a penny. You could call that failure. It *was* failure!

But in addition to the many examples of forgiveness and restoration in the Bible, there are the words of the prophets and the promises of Jesus. One of my favourite books in the Bible is Isaiah. When I became a Christian, I read John's Gospel, and Isaiah. I'm not sure why I chose Isaiah, but I certainly found wonderful promises there, as well as striking, detailed, vibrant pictures of Jesus, not least in the suffering Servant passages. I could give so many examples, but the setting is of a disobedient nation coming under judgement, yet followed by chapter after chapter of restoration. Even before the main restoration passages are reached, there is a lovely glimpse of the future. Chapter 35 speaks of the desert blossoming like a rose, and of an exiled people being restored in their land. Chapter 40 takes up the desert theme again. God's people shall return from exile through the desert, where the way will be made easy for them. Obstacles such as hills shall be made low, and difficulties such as valleys shall be raised up. When God forgives, he also restores.

1983 saw me in a place of exile, almost literally. I sometimes told people I was living 'in exile', about twelve miles distant from my wife and family. From February until the autumn of that year, I tried to attain reconciliation, believing that that was the godly way forward. But to no avail. I felt I was also in a place of exile from my Heavenly Father, though he demonstrated in many ways that his forgiveness was real. He led me (and I do not use those words lightly in the way that I sometimes feel they are tagged onto an account of an action, in order to justify it) to open a branch practice, that involved a substantial investment of money that I just did not have; he significantly increased my income to cover the maintenance payments to my wife; he asked me to do the near-impossible and open a Christian bookshop; and he guided and welcomed me into a Bible believing church where they asked me to lead worship and preach on occasions.

So how are these matters related to my financial history? Because we cannot separate our finances from the rest of our life. The Lord does not deal with our finances as though they are in a watertight box - they are an integral part of our whole life.

I had five years of relative austerity during which I came to know the Lord better, and during which I learned to give him priority; to put him first in everything, as far as I could and by the grace of God. My first five years working as a dentist could have been much more lucrative, but I sought to follow the way the Lord led me, and was fulfilled and joyful with my income and quality of life. It was all part of following Jesus, and prioritising him with regards to my finances was, in fact, just part of trying to prioritise him in every aspect of life.

Moving to Norwich was not motivated by any idea of great financial gain. In fact, I was expecting to be satisfied with a relatively low income, in view of the finance company's assessment of the practice as a 'dead duck'. And they were quite correct in pointing out that the practice had not provided my predecessor with a huge income.

And then the Lord stepped in with a miracle. Of course, unbelievers, sceptics and cynics will call it a coincidence. They have to! But after seeking to follow Jesus faithfully, and putting him first in a period of austerity, and after that of below average income, he then showed me that he is a God of abundance. This brought new challenges and new lessons to learn.

My shortcomings in dealing with my new rather affluent financial situation were but a small part of a larger problem, namely that of not wholeheartedly following the Lord. I did not turn my back on the Lord, but continued with times of Bible reading and prayer every day. And so often, during that time, he told me to repent and follow him wholeheartedly. The Lord wants us either hot or cold, and never lukewarm. The result was that the wealth that had been so graciously poured out to me, was now taken away. This brought me back to the Lord.

Which brings me to the next chapter in my life, which was one of restoration. My finances were included in this, but not to the extent that I had known during the previous six or seven years.

* * * * *

My wife and I had separated in late December 1982, and I had moved in with the afore mentioned Christian family in February 1983. I had bought a small cottage in May 1983. How, you may ask, if I had no money? I believe several miracles were involved, and that the Lord clearly knew the future (of course he does) though it was totally unknown territory to me. Let me tell you about the provision of my little cottage.

I was hoping that there would be a reconciliation with my wife, and that we would step out into a new future with our family intact. Hoping? Well, praying, fasting, receiving counselling, and so forth. But I felt it would be prudent to buy a property. If I was unsuccessful in restoring the marriage and family, I would have somewhere to live. If I was successful, then the property could be sold, or let out to tenants. But I had hardly any money.

I contacted every estate agent I could find, and asked them for details of inexpensive, small country cottages. However, weeks passed, and I received details only of bungalows and terraced houses in the city. So I decided I would have to buy a terraced house, when... There it was. A photograph in the local newspaper. A beautiful little cottage, with red roses adorning the front. It resembled a dolls house. It was not too expensive. I applied for details, and a day or two later, was being shown round.

It was small. Although there were three bedrooms, one was minuscule. Also, there was no proper bathroom (as I understood bathrooms), but a bath, wash basin and toilet at the back of the kitchen, with a floor to ceiling screen in front. It was around seven miles from where I was now lodging, attending church, and rapidly making friends, seven miles from my city practice, and seven miles from where my children lived with their mother.

There were problems, however. It had been on the market for less than a week, and already three people had put in offers to buy it. Offers of more money than I could raise. In addition to that, there was a national mortgage famine, resulting in a loosely binding agreement between banks and building societies that those applying for a loan would have to wait three months, and deposit a minimum of ten per cent of the amount themselves. I did not have sufficient funds even for the deposit, but felt I should make a bid.

And suddenly, there were unexpected surprises. Or one could say, quoting a once Archbishop of Canterbury, 'when we pray, coincidences happen'. My bid was the lowest, but was accepted, as I had nowhere to sell first. The couple selling gave me the name of a building society manager who they felt would be helpful. He offered me a 100% mortgage, and told me I had jumped the queue and would not have to wait three months for the money. Wow - everyone else got a maximum 90% mortgage and *had* to wait three months. Why was I being treated differently than the rest of the population of the UK? Answer - the building society manager was the son of the couple selling, and "I'm looking after my parents by looking after you".

I was unsuccessful in saving the marriage, and moved into the cottage in September 1983. I furnished it from a secondhand shop, except for two items of sentimental value; a standard lamp from my maternal grandfather's study, and a Victorian roll-top desk in oak that I had purchased for £10 from the previous owner of my Norwich practice. I learned to cook, launder, and keep chickens. There was grief at being separated from my family, but lovely promises daily as I read and meditated on the word of God.

My wife did not work, and there were four beautiful daughters to support. I wanted them to remain in the family home, and so gave it to my wife. But there was the mortgage to pay, and she needed to run a car. My income was described by my accountant as 'substantial', and so I drew up a legal contract whereby she would receive approximately half of my income at that time. After tax, I would have sufficient, just, to pay my new mortgage, and also pay other necessary bills. I sold my car and bought an older one! It was also larger than the previous one, so that I could transport my children in relative comfort. The car I sold had been a two-seater, and I had four daughters!

And now a curious thing happened in my finances. I was not working harder, or faster, or more efficiently, but my accountant informed me that my income had increased by around

50%. In fact, by the amount I was now giving to my wife. I had been told by several people that I was being too generous, but I did not expect the money to be returned in this manner! However, the Lord had other surprises waiting for me the following year, but in the meantime, I could enjoy my restored income.

* * * * *

"Could I come and have a few minutes of your time?" said Edwin Clement. "You might have met my wife, Jean, when you were secretary of the British Dental Association for Norfolk. She's a dentist. It's related to what I want to talk to you about".

A time was arranged and I met with Edwin.

"I'm her practice manager, really", he said. "She works in North Walsham, but started a small practice in Aylsham. Rents a room, and does one morning a week there. Waste of time now. It might have become viable, but the assistant we took on for one day a week has left, and we just want to get rid of it".

Aylsham was the town where the Christian family had shown me such hospitality and kindness. It was also where I was becoming part of a church, and gaining several good friends.

"We just want to get rid of it. No charge. So, if you would like to take the lease off our hands, it's yours. We have noticed what you've done in the city, taking one surgery to… er, how many *have* you got under that roof now?"

My heart gave a leap of joy at the prospect of having a practice in that delightful country town. I had gone there feeling *so* rejected, and the people had been so welcoming, accepting, and encouraging. But there was also a surge of adrenaline - what a step it would be in my position. Scary.

I prayed, of course. You bet I did! I had a look at the premises, being shown round by the proprietor. It was then that a mountain of a problem became apparent - he would not transfer or renew the lease. He wanted to sell.

I considered the premises. Originally a car-port between a bungalow and a garage, it had been bricked in, with a small stock room partitioned on one side at the rear, and a toilet on the other side. The main room had also been partitioned into surgery and waiting room. I wondered how much he might be asking, and whether I could possibly raise the necessary capital. And then the mountain of a problem grew out of all proportion.

"It's a job lot. Take it or leave it. There are the three properties - empty bungalow, dental surgery, and antique shop that's rented to Lovejoy. That's what I call him".

It was an impossibility. Except that - our God moves mountains, and tells us we can too. Pray? - this was top of my list, and my new Christian friends in Aylsham seemed as excited, and as prayerful, as I was. It so happened (another coincidence) that Chris, a patient who was also a friend, had just been made manager of a finance company in Aylsham. I saw my bank manager, who laughed me out of his office. "You must be joking", was almost a serious comment.

Chris knew another bank manager, and had a chat to him. I was invited for an appointment, at which I was offered a loan. I accepted, and changed banks.

My previous bank manager contacted me. "John Farmer offered you the loan? What! The swine. That's just a set-up". But I had the loan.

My accountant showed me into his office, and I told him of my new practice. And bungalow. And antique shop. He went visibly pale, and silently stared at me.

"There's a fifty-fifty chance you won't make it, you know. Especially in your present situation".

I spoke to the dentists who worked at my city practice, and explained that I would be working there half-days, five days a week, whilst doing the same at Aylsham. I started working there in March 1984. The antique dealer paid rent each week, usually, and the bungalow remained empty. I said it was too small to be called a branch practice, and referred to it as my twig practice.

Having been run as a dental practice just one half-day a week previously, how did I service the loan on the three properties, and pay the one lady that I employed as receptionist, nurse, decorator, and general fixer?

I'll say it again - when we pray, coincidences happen. There was a 'situation' in a practice not too far away, and patients flooded in. Soon I was booked solidly for three or four weeks ahead. Then a dentist a few miles away closed his practice, and moved to Europe. More patients were queueing at reception, and when I examined their teeth, I realised why he had fled. 'Fled'? - sorry, I mean 'moved'. There was a lot of treatment required by these patients.

I wanted to take my children abroad on holiday, and my nurse/receptionist wanted a car, as she travelled into Aylsham from the city on a bus each day. We worked one evening a week on 'big cases' - one man needed twenty-two teeth crowned (approved by the National Health Service) and others needed bridges. That summer, I took my children to Majorca, and my nurse bought her first car.

* * * * *

Our God does not change. He has sent prophets into this world with words of rebuke, but also words of hope, forgiveness, and restoration. The God of Joshua, Elijah and David is also the God of Barrie. Furthermore, he is your God too.

Do you know what his purpose is for you? 'Beloved, I wish that you prosper and be in health, even as your soul prospers', we read in 3 John 2. You think that applies to others, but not to you? I did. Satan whispers in our ear. 'You're not good enough, not pleasing enough, not prayerful enough, not holy enough.....'

Never write yourself off. I was tempted to do so at times. Often. There were those who sought to reinforce the enemy's words. I was even slandered (as if the truth was not bad enough) by those who were truly born again.

Stand on the word. You've let the side down? The church? People? The Lord? But surely you know that the Bible is God's inspired word. Surely you believe that when he speaks of 'cleansing from *all* unrighteousness' (1 John 1:9), he means just that. And when he says his will is to give you prosperity and health as your soul prospers, he means that too.

* * * * *

God's word is quite clear. The world might not believe it, and theologians of certain persuasions might argue against it; even ridicule it. But the Lord calls us to step out on his word. He invites us to prove him. He invites us to enter into his blessing – he delights to prosper his children. Be encouraged by my story. And if he's done it for me, he will do it for you.

* * * * *

The Bible says: *'My God shall supply all your need according to his riches in glory in Christ Jesus'. Philippians 4:19.*

Chapter 5

Sonshine After Clouds

I broke the news to my accountant. I was opening a Christian bookshop next door to my dental practice. He stared through me and said nothing for around twenty seconds or so. Then he asked me if I had a name for the shop. No, I had not, and was surprised that he thought he could help me in this way.

"I have", he volunteered. "The name is *SUICIDE*".

* * * * *

The bank manger stared at me coldly from behind his huge oak desk. Was I seriously asking for another loan? For a business that might well lose money? (And did). No, he most definitely would *not* give me a loan. But five minutes later, he had no choice, and gave me all the money I had asked for. What had happened?

* * * * *

Having bought the three units of property in early 1984, I was now looking for a tenant to lease the bungalow. The revenue would be useful in keeping me afloat financially. The practice may have been commissioned from heaven, but I needed to handle the project responsibly. A domestic tenant, residing there, perhaps? Or a commercial concern, such as the estate agents who had rented it from the previous proprietor?

However, the Lord had plans that would really blow my mind away. Plans, in fact, that would leave my accountant and bank manager thinking I was insane. That is our God.

I have always enjoyed books, and there had been times when I had romantically dreamed of owning a bookshop. Dreams that had quickly been dismissed. I was a dentist, after all. And the dreams had concerned 'nice' books, with big, shiny, attractive covers. A degree of upmarket sophistication. And even when I had considered myself reasonably well-off, I had dismissed the idea fairly quickly. But the thought did cross my mind... that bungalow... I needed to do something with it... and my accountant was obviously concerned. (Though not as concerned as he soon would be!).

I was having one of my regular prayer times, considering how good the Lord had always been, and worshipping him, when the strangest thought came into my mind. It was like a voice, though not audible. And yet so clear.

"Open a Christian bookshop, and have Dave Twidle as manager".

'How ridiculous', I thought, though I was getting that feeling again. Like when the letter had arrived about the Shaftesbury practice. Like when I had heard about the Norwich practice.

We read in the Bible of a young man called Gideon, who at one time came up with a novel way of determining the will of God. He laid a fleece on the ground, and asked the Lord to make the fleece wet with dew and the ground dry to confirm what he believed to be the will of God. The next morning it was so. To double check, he put the fleece out again, asking for the fleece to be dry and the ground to be wet with dew. And it was so. You can read about it in Judges 6. Of course, if we did this every time we had a question for God it would be a bit silly, as the Lord likes to speak to us through Scripture, by His Spirit, through anointed teachers, and so on. But being familiar with the story of Gideon, and being so impacted by what I believed I was hearing, I decided to 'put out a fleece'.

I asked the Lord that Dave Twidle might mention being a Christian bookshop manager to me. As I hardly knew him, and he was in the Air Force, I felt this would be conclusive if it happened. Can you imagine how I felt when I phoned a design studio about notepaper, Dave Twidle answered the phone (because he was on holiday, and doing some decorating there), and told me that when he shortly left the Air Force (of which I was aware), he would just love to be manager of a Christian bookshop? I was stunned.

I will not follow this through at length, as the story is covered in my first book, *THERE MUST BE MORE TO LIFE THAN THIS*. Sufficient to say that after sharing this with mature Christian friends, I felt compelled to pursue the 'project', as did Dave Twidle.

But I had no money. But my accountant felt I was already in danger of going bankrupt. But I already had a 100% mortgage on my house, and a 100% loan on my dental practice and associated property. There seemed to be so many 'but's, and no 'yet's or 'if's or 'maybe's!

Yet again, I set out for a meeting with my bank manager. I will not repeat all that's in my earlier book. Suffice to say that he listened to me, asked me a few questions, and flatly refused to give me a loan. Without a loan, I could not proceed. I needed £10,000 (worth significantly more today), and had already borrowed heavily for my house and dental property. But he was adamant.

A sudden thought. My father, a bank clerk, had spoken occasionally about LHO - Local Head Office. I knew little about how banks worked, but understood that, whilst the bank manager appeared to be the big chief to his staff and customers, there was a higher authority, the Local Head Office. I asked whether he might confirm with his LHO that my request for a loan was not acceptable, and he was agreeable. His manner suggested that his decision was an obvious one. Clearly, he felt LHO would back him 100%.

But his whole demeanour changed dramatically when he made the call, and he exclaimed loudly, "What?" My conclusion with regard to what happened, was - Jesus got there first.

So I had the loan. I made an appointment with my accountant, and although his reaction was predictable, I was taken aback when he told me to call the bookshop *SUICIDE*. He made his point.

And so *Sonshine Christian Bookshop* opened in November 1984, with Christian pop singer Dave Pope being present, and signing albums of his music for hordes of young people. Dave Twidle was manager, and there were generally volunteer helpers to assist him. My life had been lived under a cloud, perhaps many clouds, a year or two earlier. Now all that was changing, and it seemed appropriate to name the shop Sonshine, as the glorious light of the Son of God shone on me, through me, and through the work of the bookshop.

The first year, the bookshop lost £20,000. That would be a much higher figure today, allowing for inflation. In fact, well over double that amount. The shop's bank account would dip into debit, just a little, and the bank statement, when it arrived in the post, would be printed in red instead of black. The bank manager would demand to see me from time to time, but whenever money was really needed, it came in. Just once, it did not. Panic - almost. But then I found that I had a life insurance policy, still mine after the divorce had been finalised. Cashing it in brought me back into credit. Just! But that was sufficient. There was always provision, often from a surprising and unexpected source.

Some years the bookshop made a profit. Most years it made a loss, and especially when the Internet became established. It was open, serving the Christian community, and others, for twenty years. *Every* day we sold Bibles. Most days, people came in for prayer. Some came in and shared their problems. Some were really sick. Some were desperate. We got through an amazing number of tissues!

People came in and accepted Christ. People came in and were baptised with the Holy Spirit, and spoke in tongues. Perhaps more importantly, many Christians referred to it as a spiritual oasis in north Norfolk - a place where they could come and be refreshed. For *twenty years*

Dave Twidle had been an aircraft fitter, but soon demonstrated an anointing in pastoral ministry. Churches and ministers who were not of an evangelical persuasion were not always enthusiastic about the shop, but I would probably have been concerned if they were.

There were difficulties, and there was opposition. Satan does not like Christian bookshops operating on Biblical principles, and promoting the word of God. Dave and I prayed together, at least weekly, sometimes more frequently, and often with others joining us. The bank would call me in when we dipped into overdraft, but the Lord always met the need. We often did not know how the accounts would be put back into credit, and would simply go into what I called 'hilarious praise'! We just did not know what more to pray. And then there would be a financial miracle, and we would be back in credit.

We heard that there was a witches coven meeting around four miles from the bookshop, and that they were praying *against* the work of the shop. We heard that several times from several people. Probably, the coven wanted us to hear that. In Jesus Name, we have victory. Thus we prayed, and the work continued, as people continued getting saved, delivered, etc.

And then there were rumours about me. I had backslidden in some ways a few years earlier, and that gave fertile ground for gossip. One or two church leaders forbade their members from coming to the shop. But only one or two, and following a lunch with those leaders, everything was clarified and resolved.

* * * * *

"Your bookshop has not made an overall profit?" commented a professing Christian of somewhat sceptical inclination. "So it wasn't God who called you to open it in the first place, was it".

What a curious statement to make. The Bible is full of stories, all from real life, where people are called to do unreasonable things in the eyes of the world. I have already alluded to Joshua marching round Jericho in silence, Elijah drenching wood with water prior to praying that the Lord would set it ablaze, and of David facing an armed giant, with only a sling and five stones. The Lord calls his people to do irrational things, launch out into irrational projects, and pray irrational prayers. Making a profit is totally irrelevant. The crucial factors are, firstly, hearing the Lord. Secondly, obeying him.

The concept of the Christian bookshop was irrational anyway. They rarely showed a profit, unless they were part of a group, or had some outstanding feature. For me, in my situation involving stretched finances and impending divorce, that irrationality was compounded. So what? - that is our God.

Please note well - the Lord prospered me. I always had enough money to meet all my needs, and there was always money over. Our God has promised us that, and you can be assured that *our God always keeps his promises*. Sometimes there was very little money over. Sometimes there was quite a lot more. I had not been promised overflowing wealth, and nor have you. We have been promised prosperity - every need met, plus *more*. And as we walk with the Lord, listening to him, trusting him, and seeking to please him, he delights to prosper us. We do not need to worry or be anxious - prosperity is assured.

Between the years of 1984 and 2004, the bookshop lost around £115,000. Did it collapse? No. Did I experience financial hardship? No. Did it cause me to fall to my knees and cry to God at times? Yes, and that was not a bad thing to happen!

Without the bookshop, would I have been £115,000 better off? Maybe. But would the Lord have prospered my dental work if I had disobeyed him with regard to opening the Christian bookshop? We do not know.

But what I do know is this. Nothing, nothing, nothing compares with knowing the presence of God in our lives, and of the abundant joy and fulfilment of working with him. I would do it again. He has always looked after me, and he always will.

It is unlikely that you, the reader, will be called to do precisely what I was called to do. But do not limit the Holy One of Israel (Psalm 78:41). When he calls us to work with him, he provides for that work, and he provides for us. For you. For me. That is our God. That is his Word. Trust him, and you will prove him.

* * * * *

Most of my life has been full of joy. I can't say that life has always been kind to me, but that is not where I look for joy. The world seems to offer so much, but those who seek fulfilment there find that it never delivers. The new car, the new television, the latest IT gadget, the holiday that was always dreamed of – none of these things delivers the anticipated and hoped for satisfaction. That is only found in a relationship with God through the Lord Jesus Christ.

I had enjoyed life with my wife and family, and the children and I missed each other, though we spent as much time together as possible. We have lovely memories of holidays, Christmases and suchlike, and decades on, continue to reminisce together.

A new chapter of my life started with the Aylsham practice, and the Christian bookshop. I told people that I was a man who 'sold holy books and filled holey teeth'. There was an article on me in a newspaper, which started, 'In Aylsham, Norfolk, heaven and hell exist side by side'. After a few years, I sold my Norwich practice to one of my associates there, and used the money to extend the small cottage that had become 'home', and also bought a new car which would serve me for more than thirteen years. There was now much more comfortable accommodation for my daughters and other guests. The Aylsham practice had taken off from the start, and now had three surgeries.

Romance blossomed, and in 1986 I remarried. We just loved being together, and I started taking extended weekends in order to maximise shared time. We both worked in the dental practice, and sometimes in the bookshop. We were both very involved in the work of our church in the town, and holidayed in Europe, and the UK. The children joined us for a couple of weeks away each summer. There were some issues relating to my wife's mental and emotional health, and when these really kicked in, we had cottage holidays in the UK instead of going abroad. And just occasionally, my wife could not travel at all.

Financially, we just about got by, and I occasionally went back to working a five-day week. We were never ever in need, but for twenty years I was supporting my previous wife, who never remarried, and my four lovely daughters. And there was that bookshop! In addition to supporting so many of us, plus *Sonshine,* there was the expense of running our own home. I kept the same car for over thirteen years, and though we rarely holidayed in hotels, we certainly had good times. We sought to put Jesus first in our finances, giving to the work of our church, trying to be generous where we could, and once more, there was that bookshop. There was very little to save for the rainy days, but then, with Jesus, there were not too many rainy days.

After around twenty years of supporting my previous wife and children, my fourth daughter went to University, and in fact, made her home with me. That was a joy, as indeed had been the prolonged stay of my second daughter a few years earlier. At last I was free to stop maintenance payments, not least as my previous wife had a career of her own that she had been pursuing for some years. There was now surplus cash, which I had not known for a couple of decades, and it seemed that the future was all plain sailing. In a very few years I would be retiring. My wife was keen to cruise the Atlantic, sail round the Caribbean, and on to Brazil. Of course we would, if that was what she wanted. I was keen to renew the tiles on part of the roof, that had never been quite the right colour.

However, life can take some unpleasant turns at times. Little did I realise the heartbreak and financial devastation that would so quickly and unexpectedly come upon me. As I have written earlier, we don't always know what's round the corner, but I praise God that we can always know *Who* is round the corner.

* * * * *

Postcript

All my books are available at *Amazon.co.uk*, where there is also the facility for reviewing them. Back in 2012, I was not sure that I was really going to write a book, but after just three weeks of typing, and many more of editing, the manuscript of *THERE MUST BE MORE TO LIFE THAN THIS* was sitting on my desk. I had not expected any traditional publisher to seriously consider offering me a contract, but the first one I approached did just that. Suddenly, I was an author. Before long, emails and letters started arriving from people who had walked into a bookshop, and 'the title of your book just leapt off the shelf at me'. At the same time, reviews started appearing on Amazon. Some were by people who knew me, and all were favourable until… a gentleman, writing as a Christian, was sarcastic about the book. I had not written a book before, and was quite shocked at what he wrote, especially his attitude and scathing words. Maybe I was naïve, or too sensitive. I vowed I would never write another book, and felt completely nonplussed that a brother (or was he?) could write in that manner. However, I got over it!

He commented on the bookshop, and obviously saw it as a non-event. The incident where the bank manager refused me the loan, only to find his local head office telling him to give me the money, is described by this man in the following way - 'the kind of financial model that bankrupted our country'.

Surely the reviewer missed the whole point, in that the bank manager was very prudent in his judgement. However, the Lord had commissioned the shop, and *he* then facilitated the type of loan that, in *other* situations, did virtually bankrupt our country. But he also provided for me in such a way that ensured that the bank never lost a penny.

The words of the reviewer were that the Christian bookshop opened, courtesy of a bank loan on 'the kind of financial model that bankrupted our country and… it makes a loss and closes'. Why do so many people believe that unless a project makes money, it is not of God? The bookshop eventually closed, but only after serving, mainly the Christian community, for twenty years. I may not be an outstanding author, and the book reviewed was my first, but I still feel a sense of shock at the worldly values implicit in this man's review.

The Lord called the most unlikely person to set up a Christian project, which was in many respects, a mission. It was impossible, according to the ways of the world, and yet the Lord provided. That provision was considered by many to be miraculous. Through the ministry of the bookshop, people were saved, baptised in the Holy Spirit, healed, encouraged, set free, heard the Lord call them into ministry and mission, bought Bibles and Christian books…. *over a period of twenty years*. Although the shop made a substantial loss, the Lord sustained it and also looked after me. Eventually it closed, like the majority of Christian bookshops with the arrival of the Internet. I am only too aware of my own inadequacies and shortcomings, but - let's give the Lord the glory due. Sonshine Christian Bookshop was a miraculous act of God from beginning to end.

If the Lord can use someone like me, then I'm sure he can use someone like *you*, the reader. Not in exactly the same way as he used me, but - the Lord has a purpose and a call for you, and the values and limitations of this world should never hold you back.

* * * * *

The Bible says, *'The foolishness of God is wiser than men; and the weakness of God is stronger than men'. 1 Corinthians 1:25.*

Chapter 6

Plundered

We had been married many years, and yet my wife was still beautiful and vivacious, and the chemistry continued to have me tingling whenever I was with her, or even thought of her. Which was often.

"I know how much you love me, and I love you too. More than I could ever have dreamed", said the beautiful lady. And then she started to tremble, as she stuttered out, "But you see, I am *in love* with another man now".

And so started a chapter of my life that was diabolically dark, and beyond which I could not imagine anything other than mere existence. And yet...

* * * * *

It was such a shock. The love between us had been so real, and in some respects continued. For over fifteen years of marriage we had regularly written love letters to one another, even though we were together most of the time. I brought her flowers every week, and strawberries once a fortnight. Even when spending an evening at home together, she would wear make-up and dress in clothes that she knew I found attractive. She was sixteen years younger than me but would tell people, "I have got to die first, because I just couldn't live without him".

But now she *did* want to live without me. Or did she? She moved out into a rented house, and divorce papers arrived a few days later. However, she would often phone, or call round for a cup of tea, and tell me how much she loved me. I made it clear she could return, unconditionally, at any time. She continued working in the Christian bookshop, but when I left strawberries there for her, I received a letter from her solicitors accusing me of harassing her. So I stopped giving strawberries. Then she arrived with a gift for me; a pewter tooth fairy with the words *LOVE, LOYALTY, FRIENDSHIP* engraved around the base. I asked if she was returning to me, but she said, "No. Just a present for you. I thought you'd like it". Again I suspected her past mental issues were a significant factor in all that was happening. So, when she called in for a cup of tea, I would entertain her, but otherwise not. And one day it was all over. A brief appearance in court, where financial issues were finalised, and she was free and flying over the Atlantic to marry her cyber-lover.

Was it the Internet, or the mental health issues, or was it a scheme that had gone sadly wrong? Will I ever know? In fact, as the years have passed, the memories have faded and there are no important questions. Some of my readers might need to know that themselves some day. I hope not.

Financial issues had to be finalised. I prayed, and so did my Christian friends. I was so concerned for my wife - what was she getting into, and what sort of future would she have, and how would her health be affected by these things? I prayed for *her*, and so did our Christian friends. I am sure that many of them prayed for me too. My preoccupation with her welfare caused me to ignore my own, and it was only days before the court appearance that I realised that, having proved God during twenty years of supporting family, ex-wife and bookshop, I was going to perhaps have a more serious situation very soon. Losing virtually everything and having to start again at the age of fifty-seven years is hardly a viable proposition. Prayer is catalysed by such circumstances, but one does need to remember the wonderful promises we have from our Heavenly Father. They stand during good times and bad times. He is unchanging, and so are his promises.

The reader will probably be aware that responsibility, guilt, etc. is not taken into consideration at all when a married couple divorce in the UK. Certainly, that was the case in 2001/2002. Everything we had was deemed to be jointly owned, and therefore split 50/50. I had our home valued, the dental practice valued, the bookshop valued, and our cars valued. I had accrued some investments (not a fortune), and these were declared. I had likewise invested for my wife, but hers seemed to have disappeared. I even did a valuation of our furniture, causing my barrister to say, "You are the most honest man I have ever met". I was trying to cope emotionally, and mumbled something about that being my nature, as I was a born-again Christian. She did not respond to my words.

Does that seem dire? Then wait till they come to the pensions! I had set up pensions for my wife, but mine were, apparently, more substantial. Some had been running for a decade or more before I even met her. Barristers haggled, passing from room to room, negotiating with one another and their respective clients. I would soon be retiring, and so my wife took less than fifty per cent of my pensions. But because of that, she had the greater share of our other assets. I will always be indebted to my financial adviser, Scott Pinching, for being at my side, and exuding wisdom.

The dental practice was sold, and all the proceeds, which seemed a fortune, sped their way across the Atlantic. I was expecting to sell it sometime soon, and to use much of the proceeds to pay off my mortgage. Not only was that not going to happen now, but in order to raise the sum equivalent to 'half of the value of our joint assets', I had to remortgage the house for a further six figure sum. This too winged its way over the Atlantic. But my home was important to both me and my children. We all loved the place, and today I also have nineteen grandchildren exploring staircases and corridors and cupboards - and loving it. It has been extended significantly since I first moved into what some people described as 'a pretty little dolls' house of a cottage', and I have overheard more than one grandchild calling it "the best house in the whole world".

Now I had no dental practice, and twice the mortgage. Thank you Lord, for so many promises concerning your love, kindness and provision. I worked for the new owners, earning a lot less to pay a mortgage that was a lot more.

I still had the bookshop, and the bookshop still made losses. But this was part of God's call on my life, and he would sustain it.

Three of my four daughters suddenly arrived that Christmas (my wife received her divorce, technically, on Christmas Day 2001) and filled the house with laughter and joy. Daughter number four came just after Christmas, but then New Zealand is a long way from which to travel.

Plundered! That is what it felt like. What had I done to deserve it? But we can waste time feeling sorry for ourselves, and I continue to praise and thank the Lord for upholding me and giving me strength during that challenging time. I made a point of reading a psalm a day, during five different daily sessions; the same psalm during each session, reading, meditating, praying. Maybe not psalm 119 all in one go, because it has 176 verses, but generally a psalm a day. And it was as though the Lord was breathing strength and joy into me, encouraging me and giving hope for the future.

Then, one evening, whilst in prayer, I felt he said to me, "I'll give you a better life, and I'll give you a better wife". I shared this with a few friends, who gently told me that this was wishful thinking, as they knew how special my marriage had been, and also that I had been virtually cleaned out. Devastated. Plundered.

I did not know what was round the corner, but I was still quite clear about *Who* was round the corner. And I would never have dreamed of the wonderful surprises that lay in store for me.

* * * * *

The Bible says, *'The righteous cry out, and the LORD hears and delivers them from all their troubles. The LORD is near to those who have a broken heart, and saves those who are crushed in spirit'. Psalm 34:17,18.*

'My God shall supply all your need according to his riches in glory by Christ Jesus'. Philippians 4:19.

Chapter 7

Restored - and More!

My dental practice was sold, and the proceeds sent out to Canada, following on the heels of two or three pension policies that I had saved into for decades. The six figure mortgage on my home doubled as I remortgaged - in order to send another six figure sum to Canada. I retained a few investments that were protected from tax, and also my loss-making Christian bookshop.

I was fifty-seven. Would I *ever* be able to retire?

* * * * *

I sat alone in my study, praying and pondering the future. I enjoyed my work, but had assumed that I would retire one day. And I loved my patients - well, most of them - and regarded them as old friends. If I could not afford to retire, perhaps they would be friends forever!

When you have been financially plundered, in addition to the trauma and grief of losing a much-loved soul-mate, how do you pick up the pieces and continue on the journey? Of course, the answer is always Jesus, but he does require us to show some pro-activity as we walk through life with him. Sitting back and waiting for him to act can lead to disillusionment - and poverty.

Since reading through the Bible as a Christian of just four years, and writing extensive notes on every chapter for an average of three hours a night over a period of eighteen months (which one friend described as bordering on being obsessional, though I think it reflected my passion for wanting to know the truth about *all* things), I had been convinced that the Lord wants his people to prosper. Following that mammoth and significant time of study, I had read through the Bible cover to cover, quickly, several times. My conclusions were confirmed - despite the reality of setbacks, trials and challenges in the lives of all those who live in this fallen creation, the Lord desires that his people enjoy success. Biblical prosperity. Every need met, and to spare.

Alone in my home, except when entertaining guests, or when my youngest daughter was home from Cambridge University, I spent considerable amounts of time in praise and worship (I play guitar, after a fashion), Bible reading, Scripture meditation and prayer. What was the way forward? I felt I should draw up a list.

I have always used lists. For the past forty years, I have employed a diary system that involves a daily 'to do' list. If an item does not have a tick by the end of the day, it is carried over to the next day. I love ticks. If an item is unticked, I feel uncomfortable. So writing an item in my diary ensures it gets done.

I sat down with a blank sheet of paper, and considered a list of items needing to be ticked, if I was to financially recover. Where does one start? - one starts with Jesus, of course. And so item number one was 'Put God first'. And before continuing, I considered what that meant. What was the practical outworking of putting Jesus first?

3 John 2 tells me that my soul needs to be prospering in order for the rest of my life to be prospering. So, maintaining a living relationship with my Heavenly Father is paramount. Spending

a little longer in worship, Bible reading and prayer helps prosper us, whereas cutting down on devotional time *in order to spend longer working – and earning,* can have the opposite effect. Certainly on quality of life. Another aspect of putting God first is to give financially to the Lord and his work before paying one's bills or spending on other things. This is just one more of those areas of life where we are called to do something that the world finds stupid. Like approaching Goliath with a sling and a stone. Or drenching wood with water and believing it will miraculously catch fire. And yet, one doesn't put the Lord first financially in order to receive, as though one is applying a formula, or putting a ticket in a machine in order to get something out. Rather, one is being consistent concerning one's faith and relationship with the Lord. Someone once told me that he had recently been tithing (because he had been taught that tithing results in the Lord rewarding you financially), but "It does not work". Exactly. We do not give in order to get. We give as a natural outworking of our relationship with the Lord, and as an expression of gratitude for all he does for us. And we put him *first*

The rest of the list concerned practical ways in which I could maximise my income. Dental work is generally paid by the amount of treatment carried out, and I had always spent time talking to my patients and listening to them. They were friends. So item number two was 'Don't talk so much'. I would always talk with my patients, but I needed to be mindful of the cost.

Other items included staying fit, in order not to have time off sick. A healthy diet and exercise were necessary. For how long would I need to continue working? Having said that, I enjoyed my work and loved my patients. I did not know how many more years I would need to work, and so it was necessary to have a good relationship with the young dentists who had bought the practice, and for whom I now worked.

Finance had always interested me, and since being in my twenties I had read the finance and business sections of newspapers daily. I had never speculated on the stock market. To speculate is to look for a quick profit, or a fast buck. To speculate is to gamble, in my opinion. Perhaps much of life is a gamble, but one can reduce the odds, whether one is crossing the road or looking for a future income. If one is not going to get rid of all one's income by giving and spending (and some people have to, of course), there will be money to save. Somewhere. Somehow. This is a big subject, and there are Christians with very strong, and opposing, usually legalistic, views on these matters. Over the years, I had *invested*. The Lord had blessed these investments, and though I had only a modest amount (because for the previous twenty years there had been little money to invest or save in any way), I asked for wisdom from above with regard to future investment. I was hoping that there would be times when I would have something to invest.

And then there was a truly wonderful divine intervention, and life took an unexpected turn. Once I had realised that my previous marriage was over, and the divorce had gone through, I knew that I would like to be married again. Other divorcees told me I was crazy, but I don't think I was so different from many others in this respect. Was man made to be alone? I was alone, and I knew that with the right lady in my life, I would be more fulfilled. So being both spiritual, maybe, and intelligent, possibly, I asked the Lord to send a rich widow my way. There was laughter from heaven, and some time later on a Sunday morning, a lady walked to the front of our church and spoke of the fulfilment she had enjoyed since making her life around Jesus, her church, family and home. I noted that she was single. Could she be a rich widow? I telephoned, and invited her out to a restaurant. And a week later I realised that she had even less than me, having brought up two daughters with little help from a long departed husband. But we saw more and more of each other, love blossomed, and we married on the first anniversary of our first date.

Over three hundred people came to the wedding, and after the service, the church building was quickly transformed into a restaurant for a buffet reception. I used what little money I had left for a honeymoon on safari. We did not do the optional extension of a beach holiday, but a safari had been on Wendy's dream list. I still consider it to have been my best holiday ever.

Wendy was clearly gifted in the area of hospitality. And cheerfulness. Despite us both having full-time employment (Wendy was a nurse), we regularly had groups of Eastern European Christians staying with us. They were on exchange visits, or doing courses at our church. We never asked for any payment or help with accommodating and feeding them, as we always had more than sufficient. Our incomes reminded me of the widow's jar of oil in 1 Kings 17. As long as she kept pouring the oil out, the Lord kept pouring it in. She always had more, and she always had enough. Wendy received promotion after promotion until she was managing the nursing home. I had had a mission statement for my life for years before I knew Wendy. It runs, 'I am on this Earth to please God and make my wife's dreams come true'. So what were her dreams, in addition to that safari? We holidayed in the Galápagos Islands, visited the Great Wall of China, trekked in the Amazon basin, and after recalling a boyhood dream of my own, cruised to the Antarctic and walked amongst the penguins there.

By human standards, the bookshop's financial resources were precarious. However, the Lord always sustained the work, which was kingdom work. A misunderstanding with regard to redundancy left me with a bill of a few thousand pounds at a time when I could hardly afford to pay it. But the Lord provided, and the bookshop continued. There was also a strange incident concerning 'constructive dismissal'. He was a Christian and such a decent man. I never understood the problem, but I again had to put my hand in my pocket for a significant sum of money that I could ill afford. Once more, the Lord provided. The man walked away and I never saw him again. But the work of the shop continued.

On another occasion, an insurance policy set up to safeguard a family member, matured, and my financial advisor congratulated me on being about to receive seventy thousand pounds that would be a substantial help at a time of distinct challenge. It then transpired that the policy had been written in favour of another person. I telephoned them, and congratulated *them* on their good fortune. They were surprised, and said the money was 'morally' mine (their words) and they wanted me to have it. No problem. Thank you very much. And then they changed their mind, and told me over the phone they had decided to split it with me, and keep 50% themself. No problem. Thank you very much for 50%. A week later they phoned again and said they had taken financial advice and would be keeping 100% of the sum. So I thanked my Heavenly Father that he always looks after me, and asked him to bless the person who now had the money.

Wendy and I were about to be married, when I received quite a shock. The two dentists working at my practice had been working extremely hard in order to save towards buying it from me. Fifty per cent of their turnover was paid to me as 'rent'. I had no idea just how much they were earning, and paying me, as I was passing so much on to my ex-wife as her payment from the divorce. And then, just before our wedding, I received a tax bill for an additional amount due to my income being higher than expected. Sixty thousand pounds! But I had nothing like that in my account. However, the same week, Wendy sold her house, and though it was a small property with a mortgage to pay off, she received a cheque for

- guess how much? Sixty thousand pounds. It is quite amazing the coincidences that occur when you have a Heavenly Father such as we have. "Go on. Take it", said Wendy with a huge smile. How could I, when she had probably never had *sixty* pounds to her name before? But she insisted I have it as a gift, which is Wendy's nature completely. Suffice to say that I did indeed take the money and pay the tax bill, but also that the Lord enabled me to repay the sum some time later. What a God we have. And what a lovely generous wife!

One of my daughters had been with a mission in Bosnia for a number of years, working with various challenging people groups, and she told me that until she became engaged, I was her most frequent visitor. Then Herman took the number one spot. I had always been fascinated by Eastern Europe, but had only visited as a tourist, to Hungary and the Czech Republic. Then opportunities came along, through a church connection, and we travelled several times to Serbia, Latvia, and briefly, Estonia and Bulgaria. We spoke in various churches there, taught on a modular theology course, and generally enjoyed being with the people. Other people from our church went there on occasion, and whereas at least some did so with financial support from the church, we financed ourselves one hundred per cent, and generally took cash with which to bless the people there. I think it must have been obvious to people that, although I had been so plundered a year or two earlier, we had a Heavenly Father who really looked after us, such that we were in no way a financial drain on the work of the church, either at home or abroad. Likewise when we gave up a fortnight's holiday in Borneo in order to help with the work of a church in Mexico. Not only were we able to self-finance every aspect of that time, but also witnessed the most spectacular miracle that the two of us had been personally involved with. You can read about that in *THERE MUST BE MORE TO LIFE THAN THIS* and *THE CURIOUS CASE OF THE CONSTIPATED CAT*, two of my earlier books.

After twenty years of serving, mainly, the local Christian community, Sonshine Christian bookshop closed in 2004. It was almost sold, and then the sale fell through at the last minute. Bookshops were struggling with competition from large online retailers. The stock was either sold at a discount of seventy-five per cent or given away. The premises were sold, which helped a little in reducing the mortgage. The way the Lord had sustained the shop, and me, for twenty years was amazing. The shop lost around £115,000, but I was never without life's necessities. I ran the same car for over thirteen years, and enjoyed the vehicle. My daughters did too, and two of them asked me to drive them to church in it when they married. It was not posh, but it was special to us.

Church started meeting in our home, following a vivid dream in which we both felt strongly that the Lord was telling us to leave the fellowship and movement of which we had been a part for more than twenty years, and do something new. To meet in our home, in fact. Soon we were feeding people every Sunday lunchtime. I became president of a Christian businessmen's fellowship, and once a month, we had a dining room full for dinner. Never more than thirty-five! Wendy continued to cheerfully plan, cater, serve and laugh. As fast as money flowed out, it flowed in again, and faster, and more. Investments increased, sometimes fivefold. Our six-bedroomed home was so often full. We had parties for people in the village, inviting one hundred or more, and entertaining perhaps sixty. Through the parties, our circle of friends widened significantly. One lady came to faith, and others came to Full Gospel dinners and similar. Although some of my pensions had flown to Canada, we retired, and life became even busier. And more fun. To me, the sums did not seem to add up, as we entertained the masses, and travelled around the world (six daughters in five different countries).

What an amazing Heavenly Father we have. What an adventure life can be when we set out with Jesus. What prosperity we can know when we learn from both our failures and successes, and seek to live by the principles we find in the Bible. What fun indeed.

And so today, in our sixteenth year of marriage, and with me in my seventy-fourth year of life, I reflect on the lavish generosity of an amazing God, and would like to share with you some of the lessons and principles learned concerning prosperity and success.

Finance is an adventure. And the adventure continues!

* * * * *

The Bible says, *'God is able to make all grace abound toward you, that you, always having all sufficiency in all things, may have an abundance for every good work'. 2 Corinthians 9:8.*

PENNIES FROM HEAVEN
PART TWO
* * *

*How to get them,
and what to do with them!*

Chapter 8

Pennies - How to Get Them!

"It's obscene. That's what I call it. *Obscene!*" said a rather indignant lady in the queue at the local supermarket. She was speaking to the woman next to her, but immediately commanded a far wider audience. Everybody was listening.

Was she referring to the language used in so many television programmes, films, books, newspapers, and the world of entertainment generally these days? No, though I would describe much of it that way.

Was she referring to sex scenes shown on television, the Internet and in movies these days, and which children of a young age can easily view? No, though I would not hesitate to describe them as such.

She was in fact describing a footballer's salary, and in a manner that was fashionable a few years ago. I suspect that she would have used the same word to describe the incomes of many other people too, including some of the leaders of British industry, pop stars, film stars, television presenters, and so on. The word was quite popular amongst certain people of modest incomes describing those on substantial incomes. Obscene it was.

So what is a fair income, and how does one get it? People seem to find it easier to recognise what is unfair, or 'obscene', than to identify what is fair. And I suspect that most people would not settle for a fair income if they were, instead, offered one that could be described as obscene.

* * * * *

What a deliberately seductive title to this chapter! If you've come here straight from 'Contents', then examine your heart. What was your motive? But be reassured, it is God's nature to give. Look around you - creation shouts it. Consider the lilies of the field and the birds of the air. Consider the rest of creation. Go back to the beginning, to Eden, and you find it. Adam and Eve did not even consider their 'income', such as where the next meal was coming from. Our God loves to give.

Grace! There are many aspects to receiving 'pennies from heaven', but the over-riding source of our income is the grace of God. Even when man cut himself off from the Lord and was expelled from the Garden of Eden, he was still provided for. He had to work for it 'by the sweat of his brow' (Genesis 3:19), but the source of everything good was still the Lord. Adam and Eve were not working for a monetary income, but in order to eat, drink and have shelter. Their 'income' was fruit, vegetables and meat, derived from the soil and the rain. They cultivated the soil and looked after the herds, but the source was the Lord. He causes the sun to rise on the evil and the good, and rain to fall on the righteous and the unrighteous (Matthew 5:45).

The Lord has made many promises that he will provide for his people. 'The Lord is my shepherd; I shall not want' (Psalm 23:1) is quite conclusive, and also flows with the tenor of the rest of Scripture. We have a God who has promised to look after his people. "Look at the birds, and look at the flowers", said Jesus to his followers. "If your Father in heaven will make sure that the birds have food and that the flowers are clothed, will he not look after his own children?" That is my paraphrase of Matthew 6:25-34, and it tells us that concerning our day to day needs, we are cared for by a Father in heaven.

But he promises his children more than just food and clothing. In Philippians 4:19 we read that our God shall supply *all* our needs. Food and clothing plus more. And the 'more' can be wisdom, revelation, strength, health, a marriage partner and so much more. Anything that is truly a need (and some of those things I have just mentioned may not be) are covered by this promise.

There are other factors which need to be considered. We are told to be generous, and that if we are, then we will never be in need ourselves. Conversely, those who are mean with what they have will tend to struggle financially. We take a look at this in chapter 11. There are certain kingdom laws concerning sowing and reaping, though perhaps not as interpreted by some. You might like to consider my understanding of this in chapter 12. We are given wisdom and told to use it. If we do so, the effect on our income will be positive, and if we neglect it, that too can be reflected in what we receive. I deal with this in chapter 13. We are told to work, and our employment, or otherwise, will have a most significant bearing on our income. I write concerning this in chapter 14. But the backdrop to all this is the grace and goodness of God. Having our needs met does not depend on just this one scripture, but on the whole revelation of Scripture concerning who our Father is, and of his nature. The Lord has always been good to those of his children who have 'walked in his ways'. And yet his provision for us can be taken a step further, from food and clothing and all other needs, because in many places prosperity is mentioned. 3 John 2 states it emphatically, and I have quoted this scripture several times already. Psalm 1 also talks about success in all things, and so do many other scriptures. It is our Father's pleasure to prosper us, and give us success in this life. That is his word, and that should be the experience of those who walk by faith, really believing the word, and who also live lives pleasing to the Father.

* * * * *

There are two aspects to receiving our 'pennies from heaven', namely living in faith that our Heavenly Father will be providing for us, and secondly, living our lives in a manner that pleases him. Now, do not misunderstand and feel that if we live our lives according to his desire, we will then earn his favour and be rewarded with income. That is not how any aspect of our salvation works. But if we are walking in the goodness and provision of our Heavenly Father, then we will be grateful for that, which will be reflected in our attitude and conduct.

All aspects of our salvation are received by grace through faith, and our salvation involves a lot more than being taken off the road to hell and being placed on the road to heaven. After we have left this life, either through bodily death or by meeting Jesus in the air at the rapture, we will receive a new eternal and immortal resurrection body, and will enjoy health, joy and completeness in every way. That is what was intended at the beginning, and that is where the Lord is taking those who have trusted in him. That is our salvation in the future, but it starts the moment we put our trust in Jesus.

Furthermore, we get a big foretaste of what is to come even while we are in this life on Earth. We are told that receiving the Holy Spirit into our lives is a 'down payment' (Ephesians 1:14). In some Bibles this is translated as 'earnest', which means the same, but in old English. The joy I sense within my being as I sit at my desk writing this, is a foretaste of heaven. When the Lord healed my irritable bowel syndrome around twenty or more years ago, that was a foretaste of heaven. The health and energy I enjoy today in my seventy-fourth year of life, is a foretaste of heaven. Likewise, being provided for financially in this life is part of our salvation, and a foretaste of heaven.

But what are the practical mechanics of receiving pennies from heaven. As our income is part of the Lord's provision for us, and an aspect of our salvation, it is received by grace through faith (Ephesians 2:8,9). That is how salvation is received. Faith comes by hearing, we read in Romans 10:17. We need to hear the Lord speak to us concerning our income and provision, and doing so creates faith. Faith is defined in Hebrews 11:1, where it is described as 'the substance of things hoped for and the evidence of things not seen'. *Substance* and *evidence*, which are so much more certain than hoping. Once we have faith in something, we have a rock-solid confidence. That comes from hearing God. Reading the promises that the Lord has given us concerning his provision, and meditating on the teaching he gives on the subject and the plain statements of fact that we find in the Scriptures, and allowing the Holy Spirit to speak them into our souls, creates faith. Surely that is how we first came to know the Lord? Hearing the Holy Spirit speak to our spirits concerning the gospel caused us to repent and trust in Jesus. In fact, unless we have faith such as is described in Hebrews 11:1 we cannot please God (Hebrews 11:6). But faith does more than please God – it opens the way into all aspects of our salvation.

* * * * *

In the chapter entitled *Promises, Promises!*, I have listed some of the promises that the Lord has made to his people. Read them, and then read them again. In fact, read them to be familiar with them, meditate on them and listen for God. When the Holy Spirit takes a promise and speaks it to your heart, then you *know* it's true. Why? – because you have heard the Lord tell you. And that creates faith. Faith that is sure and certain. Faith that pleases God (Hebrews 11:6).

Do not set out to use individual promises as a tool for getting finance. Allow the promises to enlighten you with regard to the nature of our Heavenly Father. Know who he is and what his character is towards his children. Then walk in faith, knowing that every need will be met, because it is his will and his nature to prosper you and give you success.

Look at it like this – the promises of God are the comfort zone within which you live. To consider not having joy, or health, or income, is foreign territory to you. The promises of God are what you expect. They are where you live. They are home, and anything else is alien. Know them. Hear them. Embrace them – and live in the experience of them daily.

Then consider the section *Responsibilities, Responsibilities*. If we have a Father who exudes grace and prosperity and success towards his children, then how should we respond? What are our responsibilities? Allow the Holy Spirit to takes these scriptures, and then walk in a manner pleasing to the Lord. Live indeed with an attitude of gratitude. Let this way of life also be home territory. To live otherwise would not be *you*. To live in any other way would be alien – you are a child of God looked after by your Heavenly Father, and you live as such.

* * * * *

To summarise, we are told to simply trust our Heavenly Father to meet all our needs. Matthew 6:25-34 tells us to consider the birds of the air and the lilies of the field, which do not worry about being fed and being clothed. If their Heavenly Father takes care of them, how much more will he look after us. A wonderful promise.

But we are also told to put the Lord first in all matters of life (Exodus 20:3. Matthew 6:33), to work (Exodus 20:9), to be generous (Proverbs 11:25), to use discernment (1 Corinthians

12:10), and to be prudent and sensible (Proverbs 14:15). These are responsibilities to be taken seriously.

Let's explore some of these aspects of prospering in the following short chapters. But firstly, what's it all about? Why does the Lord want to give his people success? Why does he want to prosper *you*? We will take a look at that in the next chapter.

* * * * *

The Bible says, *'Beloved, I pray that in all respects you may prosper and be in good health, just as your soul prospers'. 3 John 2.*

'Fear not, little flock; for it is your Father's good pleasure to give you the kingdom'. Luke 12:32.

Chapter 9

God's Purpose for You in Prosperity

We are told that we live in the *Me! Me! Me!* society, and I partly believe it. But this is nothing new, and has been a feature of human society since the Fall. The essence of sin is selfishness, where I am on the throne of my life. My decisions are based largely upon, 'what's best for me'. At elections, people vote generally for the party that will benefit *them* the most, in their opinion.

When we are born again, we start a whole new life. That is why Jesus used the expression 'born again'. He changes us, but wants our co-operation. We are labourers together with the Lord, even when it comes to building the character of Christ in us. Now Jesus is on the throne of my life - or is he? Old habits die hard, and so do old lifestyles.

The world tends to view prosperity in a selfish and materialistic manner. Luxury comes to mind, and things that are expensive. *Things*. Expensive homes, expensive furniture, expensive cars, expensive holidays, expensive clothes, expensive jewelry.... There are also sections of the Church where expensive *things* are important. There are other sections of the Church where a simple lifestyle is promoted as being godly.

Christians are supposed to live in luxury? All Christians? They should never have to live modestly? But how does that view square with Jesus himself walking Galilee, Judea and Samaria dressed simply and living modestly? Jonah, Amos, John the Baptist, the twelve disciples, the apostle Paul, Mary and Joseph, Onesimus.... My impression is that these people lived modestly, using any money they had for daily necessities. And if that was the case, had they fallen short of God's desire for them to prosper? I return once again to the definition of prosperity given by my friend Don - of needs met, and more. Just that.

Conversely, are all Christians supposed to live simply? All Christians? Should they never live in luxury? We read in the Bible of many godly people who were wealthy. Abraham, Isaac, Jacob, Joseph, David, Solomon, Philemon, Joseph of Arimathea, and many more. There were ladies who supported Jesus financially, and they are recorded in Luke 9:2,3. It is more than likely that they were reasonably well off. Were these people wrong to enjoy luxury, as some of them undoubtedly did? Did they fall short of God's heart for them to be godly? I think not.

Unregenerate man loves to have rules, because rules were made for unregenerate man (1 Timothy 1:9). To state that godly people should live modestly, or that godly people should live in luxury, is quite pleasing to those who live in one of these categories. But amongst God's people, there have always been rich and (relatively) poor. His purpose has always been that all needs should be met, plus more. There may not be luxury, but our God delights to give us more. He loves to prosper us. Why? Why prosper us? What is his purpose for the 'more'? Let us consider why the Lord wants to prosper his people.

* * * * *

Blessed to extend the kingdom.

Greg (not his real name) started life in relatively modest circumstances. He launched out in property. The Lord prospered him in that, and he then diversified. During this time, he was very upfront with his faith, and personally led innumerable people to the Lord, many of whom continue in leadership today. Although described in the press as a Christian philanthropist (which he is), I would call him an extremely generous man of God. He has given millions and millions of pounds to community and church projects, as well as helping many individuals who have fallen on hard times. His generosity is usually cloaked in anonymity. He has played a most significant part in extending the kingdom of God into both individual lives and communities, through his personal witness and use of his God-given prosperity. In addition to blessing so many people, he also endures relentless criticism from small-minded meanies who are so obviously envious at what the Lord has done for him.

Most people would describe Greg as wealthy, but he lives in Biblical prosperity both receiving and giving generously, not least in order to extend the kingdom of God.

* * * * *

Steve and Hayley (again, I have changed their names) had never enjoyed much wealth. Steve did what he knew best, which was gardening, fixing things, mending things, decorating, and most other things he might be called upon to do or lend a hand with. If there was no work, or sickness struck, government benefits were a safety net, but a last resort. However, they would testify that, even with a large family to bring up, the Lord had always blessed them with 'more than enough to meet every need'. But with regard to their finances, they put Jesus first. And they were always generous to other people.

The work of their church expanded, and the congregation outgrew various rented buildings. With virtually no money in their account, the leaders and people launched out, buying a large building that would enable them to extend the kingdom of God into many more lives and situations.

Steve and Hayley cashed in their one and only savings policy. "We put what we could aside for a rainy day", Steve told the leaders. "It's not a fortune, but we have decided that with Jesus in our lives, there won't be a rainy day. So we're giving it to be used for extending the kingdom".

Few people would describe Steve and Hayley as wealthy, but they lived in Biblical prosperity, both receiving and giving generously, and doing their bit to extend the kingdom of God within their area.

* * * * *

I have taken the examples of Greg, and of Steve and Hayley, to illustrate how the Lord prospers individuals in order to extend the kingdom. As a father myself, I know what it is to want my children to enjoy life *and* be generous to others, and I believe the Lord is pleased to see Greg enjoying a relatively lavish lifestyle, as well as so generously blessing others. I also feel I know the Lord's sentiments towards Greg's critics.

Steve and Hayley do not live a lavish lifestyle, but are full of joy and contentment, enjoying the good things that the Lord has blessed them with. All their needs are met, and they have more. They use their 'more' to bless others and extend the kingdom.

Like me, most of my readers will enjoy prosperity on a much smaller scale than Greg, and are probably closer to Steve and Hayley in that respect. But as we walk in faith, knowing the character and promises of God, and living with an attitude of gratitude such as Greg displays, we too will be putting Jesus first, *and* using 'what's left after our needs have been met' to extend the kingdom of God. There is no such thing as a perfect church, and no church is 100% efficient in the use of offerings and funds. However, 'ministers' need to be supported, and buildings need upkeep. It is easy for cynics to criticise churches, but there are so many in our city of Norwich (Norfolk, UK) preaching the gospel and seeing people respond, going out on the streets and housing the homeless and feeding the hungry, as well as seeking to meet the needs of countless people in the church, the community, the UK and the rest of the world, not least the undeveloped countries where the needs are astronomical.

People who truly respond to the gospel are changed for ever. They find fulfilment, friendship, and fellowship in this life, and an eternal destiny that will exceed their wildest expectations.

Resources that churches and individuals pour into the community enhance the lives of, especially, the poor. If evangelical Christians were somehow snatched out of this world, the impact on the poor and disadvantaged would be devastating. Secular charities, devoid of Christian support and funding, would probably collapse.

We are called to be salt, to bring flavour to this world. We are called to be light, to show people the way in the darkness. Sharing the gospel, and performing acts of kindness are the way - but financial prosperity can multiply our ability to do this. Let's walk in the promises, and enhance our flavour and light.

If giving £10 can bless a needy person, why not seek to launch out with the Lord and bless 10 needy people? If £100 given to a mission brings the gospel to a number of people, why not seek to double the giving and double the number of people reached?

Our Heavenly Father is pleased to see his children blessed in this world, but his primary desire is the extension of the kingdom of God, and the uplifting of Jesus. The Spirit seeks to honour and glorify Jesus, and the Spirit and Jesus seek to please the Father. The Father's heart is to see Jesus honoured and glorified. We are called 'co-labourers together with him' (1 Corinthians 3:9) - let us walk in the Spirit, seeking to extend the kingdom, glorify the Son and please the Father. As he prospers us, let us increase our co-labouring.

We are not called to be a part of the *Me! Me! Me!* society. We are called to be kingdom builders. Like me, you might not be a Greg, but we are called to walk in the Spirit and to walk in the promises of God, where every need is met, plus more. Let us use at least some of the 'more' to extend the kingdom and honour Jesus.

* * * * *

Blessed to be a blessing.

Chris and Mary pulled into a service station to fill up with petrol. They were careful when it came to travelling, because they needed to keep an eye on the cost. And not just travelling. They always had enough, and more. But just a little more.

"Hey, look over there", said Chris. "It's Bob Dale filling his Porsche. Not his Mercedes or Roller tonight then. God has really blessed that man. *And* I've met him a few times". Again, I have changed the names.

Chris shuffled out of the car, and whilst removing the fuel cap, caught Bob's eye. They smiled and nodded a silent 'Hello' to one another across the forecourt. By the time Chris had finished filling his elderly car, the Porsche had gone.

"Nothing to pay, sir", said the man behind the counter. "Don't know who or why, but the man in the Porsche paid your bill before leaving".

Chris felt blessed. Loved. He felt so special. And he knew that his Heavenly Father loved him.

Most people would describe Bob as wealthy, but he lived in Biblical prosperity both receiving and giving generously.

* * * * *

Norma felt the call of God on her life. She had a university degree that would have ensured security and a future within the profession she anticipated joining and working within. Now, instead, she applied to go abroad with a mission that would bring the gospel and the love of God to a needy people.

"We won't be paying you", said a mission spokesman. "You will have to have faith that the Lord will supply your every need. And first of all, find a job, and save money that will help you get started".

Norma applied to work in a tea house where she waited at tables, and, after a few months had saved the significant sum of money stipulated by the mission. She was told they would now place her with a team working abroad. Did the money she had saved help her get started with the work? No - she gave it all to the poor and homeless, knowing she could trust Jesus to provide for her as she worked for him.

Few people would describe Norma as wealthy, but she lived in Biblical prosperity, both receiving and giving generously. She had been blessed, and now she was blessing others - selflessly.

* * * * *

One of my favourite scriptures is the passage where the Lord speaks to Abraham in Genesis 12:1-3. The Lord made certain promises to Abraham, and the one which I have always found most meaningful was that he would bless Abraham and make him a blessing to others. I felt that passage, and especially the promise I have just mentioned, was for me too. Looking back over my life, I see the fulfilment of that promise. He has blessed me time and time again, not because I deserved it but because of his grace and mercy and kindness. That is who our Heavenly Father is. That is what he does. And his blessing on his people enables us to bless others.

The Lord blessed Abraham and made him a blessing to others. His family was blessed. His household was blessed. His community was blessed. When the community was defeated in battle and plundered by the enemy, Abraham had the blessing of God (the resources) to rout the enemy and bring back the plunder (Genesis 14:1-16).

Wherever Abraham went, the presence of God went with him. Likewise with us. Wherever we are, there will be blessing. We need to walk in the Spirit and walk in the promises of God - and we will take prosperity with us. My dental practices grew and grew, as I added surgery after surgery. The Christian bookshop grew in influence as people came to know the Lord there, and his touch on their lives in many ways. People tend to view these things in human worldly terms. One man told me, "You are OK because you are a dentist". But twice everything had been taken from me, and I knew dentists who had suffered less and yet lived in poverty. The bookshop made significant losses, and yet the work prospered. And I prospered - not because I was a dentist, but because the Lord is good.

Chris and Mary were really blessed through Bob, because the Lord had blessed Bob, and his heart was to bless others. How about you? Norma knew that the Lord would always meet her needs, and more, and when she had 'more', she used it to bless people in need, as an expression of God's love and of his kingdom.

Think back to Greg in the first section of this chapter. Innumerable people have been blessed through Greg. But that is because the Lord has blessed him, and Greg wants to bless others. Are you seeing the principle? It is not that Bob, Steve, Hailey, Greg or Norma have felt, 'I suppose I ought to give to others now'. No - I know these people, and others like them. Their attitude is, 'Hey, now I can bless others. Where shall I start? How much can I give, and to whom?'

I have been in a number of churches and fellowships where it is not unusual to find an envelope in the offering, with a person's name on it. When they open the envelope, there is usually money in it! That person is blessed financially, because the Lord has blessed someone else, who in turn wants to bless others. And as they give, so they themselves receive, according to the promise of Luke 6:38.

There may be tightfisted individuals in some churches, but frankly, they just don't belong there. Our Heavenly Father is lavish, generous, kind, etc. and wants his children, who are created in his image, to demonstrate his nature to the world. Do you? Freely? There really is no place for meanies in the kingdom of God. It's the givers who receive (Luke 6:38 again), and the withholders and tightfisted who find that the Lord is not quite so generous to them as he is to others who are testifying about it. Remember Abraham, and remember Luke 6:38.

Consider the two seas in the Holy Land. There is the Sea of Galilee, and the Dead Sea. The former has water flowing out as fast as it flows in. It is full of life. The Dead Sea has water flowing in, but nothing flows out; the water just evaporates. Nothing lives there. It is *dead*. Think about it!

When the Lord blesses you, bless others. When the Lord blesses you, keep it flowing. Why? Because he blesses you to make *you* a blessing. And the more you bless others, the more the Lord will bless you.

A witness to a watching world.

Observing the Lord's provision for his people was one factor that helped bring my wife to the Lord many years ago. Wendy was not a Christian, but others were starting to talk to her about Jesus. Then some people who lived further along the road faced a real challenge. Wendy's friend told her, "The husband has lost his job, and his wife is expecting their first child".

"How will they manage?" Wendy asked.

"They're Christians", her friend said. "They will be looked after".

Wendy was curious, and over the days that followed, enquired how the family were faring. She learnt that when there was no food, they would sit at the table and pray. Sometimes they would find food on the doorstep, and sometime money would come through the letter box. It was not angels - it was Christians. And after a while, the husband had work again. Work that paid well, and so he could start blessing others again too.

This occurrence was a significant milestone in Wendy's journey towards accepting Jesus as her Saviour and Lord. In fact, it is part of her testimony.

* * * * *

My cousin Rosemary was relating an incident that had happened to two of her neighbours. Audrey and a friend had been having lunch in a local restaurant, and Audrey was speaking about a book she had been reading. I was the author! A man sitting elsewhere in the restaurant walked over to them, and said, "I couldn't help overhearing you say that you have read a book by Barrie Lawrence. I happen to know him. May I join you for a few minutes and tell you about him?"

The stranger joined them, and told them that he had been to my home. He did not know me well, but could tell them that everything they read in my books was absolutely true. That he knew, and he wanted them to know. Then he left.

"But when I went to pay", said Audrey, "the girl at the till said that the man had paid for us already. It was not a cheap restaurant, and I don't even know his name".

But what an impression that incident made on Audrey and her friend. That stranger was clearly a man of God. And his generosity made a statement about the kingdom of God.

* * * * *

Audrey's story had me scratching my head for some weeks. Then months. Eventually I forgot it, until a friend of mine said, "I must tell you what happened to my friend Rod some time ago. He was in a restaurant down in Suffolk, and he heard two ladies discussing a Christian book. It was one of yours, Barrie. Well, Rod went over...."

Rod might not be considered a wealthy man, as some would define wealthy. But he has been prospered by God, and he freely blesses others where he sees an opportunity. And what a witness. Audrey was telling everybody about it.

Likewise with Wendy's neighbours. Who were the Christians who were leaving food and money? She did not know, but what was important was that it was happening. And the fact that people were blessing this couple, spoke volumes to Wendy.

Consider the above stories. Wendy was really amazed at two aspects of her neighbours' experience. Firstly, they were provided for. Not everybody was, and how many found food parcels on their doorsteps, or money coming through their letter box? This was a powerful witness of the living God to Wendy.

Secondly, Wendy was struck by the generosity of people who left food on doorsteps and who pushed money through letterboxes. They were Christians. She had heard nothing like this before. This too was a powerful witness.

Also, Audrey's story. This chap who came to their table was clearly a man of God. Who was he? Why had he paid for their lunch? Again, this made a powerful statement.

In each of the above cases, and in thousands of others across our nation, and across the world, ordinary people, like you and me and Rod and the people in the first story, just love to bless others because we ourselves have been blessed. There is no ulterior motive. There is no secret agenda. Because we have been blessed, we want to bless others. And a watching world looks on - and notices.

We are not meant to scrape by somehow, just paying the bills and staying afloat by the skin of our teeth. We are called to walk with the Lord, and to know his prosperity in this life; to have our needs met, and more. More - to bless others. To give. And what a powerful statement it makes. We are not meant to be like the world. We are called to be *different*. We are called to be generous. We are called to be kingdom people, demonstrating our Father's heart to this sad world.

The patriarchs of the Old Testament – Abraham, Isaac, Jacob and Joseph – along with godly kings such as David and Solomon, were witnesses to the presence and character of the one true living God. Abraham was a tremendous witness to the provision of God. We are called his children (Galatians 3:29), and we too should be witnesses to a watching world. Let us be faithful. If the Lord has prospered us, then let us show generosity to those in need. And may the world see, and take note.

Abraham was a witness. David was a witness. Solomon was a witness. So are you. Don't mess up - the world is watching.

Because he is a loving Father

Jesus told his disciples that it is more blessed to give than to receive (Acts 20:35). This is true of our God as well as his children. He loves to give. It is his loving nature to give to his children. That is why he keeps giving.

When we give, we are blessed. There is a feel-good factor, which is not selfish, but similar to the fulfilment one experiences when doing what one is good at. One could liken the experience to playing a musical instrument, or painting a picture - whatever you are gifted at. This blessedness is enhanced when one is giving to one's children. If you are a parent, what do you want for your children? Poverty? Mediocrity? We want the best. We want to see our children fulfilled, happy, and enjoying life. And we are created in the image of God. That is how he feels about us.

Don't be envious of the person who has more. The Lord has blessed them, and he looks down and is pleased. (If they are mean, selfish, etc. that is a different matter, but one should still not be envious of what the Lord has given them).

So *delight in* the blessing of God 'who gives us all things richly to enjoy.' (1 Timothy 6:17). *Richly. Enjoy.* Jesus is God, and no-one spoke more seriously about love, life, death, eternity, and God's purpose for us. But he was also someone people liked to have around. He was good company. *That* is our God. So we can bless our Father by enjoying what he has given us, whilst always being mindful of the needs of the kingdom and of the poor. *Enjoy* the blessing which makes you rich, and enables you too to bless others.

* * * * *

The Bible says, *'Teach those who are rich in this world not to be proud and not to trust in their money, which is so unreliable. Their trust should be in God, who richly gives us all we need for our enjoyment'*. 1 Timothy 6:17.

Chapter 10

Pennies – What to Do With Them!

A close family member was clearly concerned about my changing circumstances, and how I was handling life now. They asked to have an earnest heart-to-heart chat.

"It's your money", they said, looking rather tense. "I'm not at all comfortable with the amount you are spending these days. Since the practice has been doing well, you seem to be spending more and more", They hesitated before going on, but decided to see the matter through.

"And it's not just your spending", they continued. "You always saved what you could, but now you are reading about finance and *investing*. You must be saving a lot more than you ever used to. I'm not sure you've got it right".

I paused to think, but before I had a chance, they continued.

"And that's just *part* of the problem. The other thing that is bothering me is the amount you seem to be giving away these days - to the church, to missions, to individuals, to charities... You're giving so much away. I'm really concerned about it".

Silence. Time to consider. It was indeed a problem.

"I *can* spend less", I replied. "But then I will have more left, and I will have to either save it or give it away. But if I am already saving too much, then I will just *have* to spend it, or give it away. But you also feel I am giving too much away as it is. There is, in fact, only one answer. I will have to earn less".

"Never", they said. "You can't do that".

I sat down quietly and reflected. God had been good to my wife and me. We had been used to living on a modest income, because I had chosen to work somewhere that did not yield the level of income that many dentists expected. Secondhand furniture and secondhand cars were more than adequate. After some years, we had moved to a place where we felt the Lord wanted us, and where we felt we would again receive only a modest income. That was no problem as the Lord always gave us more than enough. Then, suddenly, everything changed. Amazingly and unexpectedly - but that is our God. Income poured in. It was many times what we were used to. We started spending more. With three children now (and soon four), we bought a five-bedroomed house, and our first ever *new* car. But there was so much left over. It was accumulating in the bank, but getting little interest, and so I started investigating other ways of investing money. And all this after giving increased amounts to church, missions, people in need and charities.

The person speaking was quite correct about me spending, saving and giving more - but I had to, because I *had* more! Our dramatic change of circumstance highlighted for us an issue that faces everyone, and every family. Budgeting. How much do we *spend?* How much do we *save?* How much do we *give?*

* * * * *

With regard to the question of the amount that we spend, save and give, there are varying, and strongly held opinions to be found amongst Christians. I have come across people who have felt that they should live on only the bare necessities and give everything else away, regardless of how high their income might be, and including any lump sums of cash that might come their way. There are others who feel that they should give 10% of their income to the church, and that they can apply prayerful discretion to the use of what remains. Some simply try to be generous as a lifestyle, and I suspect that there are also those who do not think about it much at all. If you are in this final group, perhaps now is the time to start.

Law and legalism appeals to unregenerate man. That is why the Old Testament is concerned with people living under the Old Covenant of the Law, whereas the New Testament speaks to a people living under the New Covenant of grace. However, bringing people out from a covenant of law is, maybe, easier than getting law out of people. Human nature loves law, and religious human nature thrives on it.

How can law rear its head in the realm of money? It does so when people state or imply that others should be doing what they do, or what they attempt to do, or what they say they do – even if it's not in the Bible. There are usually scriptures that suggest they are right, until other scriptures are put forward that suggest something else. There are Old Testament scriptures that suggest God's people should tithe (give 10% of their income to the Lord), whereas there are some New Testament scriptures suggesting that followers of Jesus should give away '*all* that they have'. There may well be other doctrines concerning giving based on other scriptures, but the two I have just mentioned are used for illustration. We each need to be clear what the Spirit is saying to us, and we each need to steer clear of condemning others, overtly or covertly, by stating that "everyone should do what I do", unless it is clearly in the Bible, and for all Christians today.

* * * * *

The Church should be leading the way for the rest of society, like a beacon in the dark. For indeed we are called to be just that. But so often it is a weak, feeble Church trotting along behind a world that has values and culture far removed from those of Scripture and the kingdom of God. When the world decides that sex outside of marriage is acceptable, there is part of the Church that will naively follow. When the world decides that killing children who are unborn, because they are a nuisance to the lifestyle of the parents, is acceptable, then there is a part of the Church that will mindlessly follow. When the world decides that other religions ('false gods' and 'abominations' in the Bible) are to be regarded as of equal status to worshipping and following the true God, there will be a part of the Church that will follow. We are told that we are to be *different* from the world. Therefore we should be transformed by the renewing of our mind, which leads to the transforming of our thinking, our values, and our behaviour (Romans 12:1-2).

Spending, saving, giving – that is the order in which most people in the world consider their money. What do they have to spend? What would they like to spend with what is left over? How much should they save? And finally, what should they give, if they do that sort of thing? That is what the world does, because that is the way the world thinks. We are called to be *different,* and if we are doing what the world does, perhaps we need to be transformed.

Giving.

Jesus should always come first. To apply this truth in the world of personal finance might be quite a challenge to those who have never thought this way before. However difficult though, we each need to consider whether we are really - *really* - putting the Lord first when it comes to our money. You might like to consider how I handled this when I was first challenged by it (chapter 1). Do you *want* to put the Lord first in your finances? *Today*? - or at some future time when you have more income and less expenditure? Who are you kidding!!!! The right time is always *Today!* Never tomorrow.

It is difficult to start putting Jesus first in your finances if that is something you have not been doing before. Your income is probably already committed to other things. Many people live to the full extent of their income, and if that income increases, the increase is used for more spending. We can all find a good reason to justify spending, and that does not mean that spending is wrong. It is an issue of priorities; namely, is Jesus coming first?

I have already said that the Church is too much like the world. The values of the kingdom of God are different from those of the world. Likewise when it comes to priorities and culture.

The world values *things*. In fact, the world puts such a high value on *things* that inessential objects and items and gadgets are considered to be absolutely essential. I am not suggesting that people should not have dishwashers, televisions, computers, mobile phones, and electronic gadgets that entertain and make life easier in a thousand ways - but none of the above are *essential*. Furthermore, people usually opt for the best that they can afford. That is not wrong in itself, unless one is a child of God, and feeling that one cannot afford to give to the Lord. Is Jesus coming first?

The culture of the world today values entertainment very highly. Hence the proliferation of so many types of television, the number of television channels, the huge variety of computer games, sport played throughout weekend mornings, afternoons and evenings as well as most other times, and so on. Recreational eating, enjoying restaurants of a multiplicity of ethnicities, has mushroomed (please excuse the pun) since

I was young. Again, these things are not wrong in themselves, but if I am a child of God and indulging in these, whilst feeling I cannot afford to give, something is wrong. Is Jesus coming first?

The priorities of the world are totally different from those of the kingdom of God. Give to God, his work and the poor? - "You must be joking!" is a likely response to your face, whilst actually questioning your sanity behind your back. The world's priorities are so different from those of the kingdom, and yet so much of the Church just follows the world. Where is the difference? Giving is not a priority - spending is *the* priority. But if that is the way I am living, I am certainly not putting Jesus first.

The laws of the world are different from the laws of the kingdom. The laws of the world are natural laws, whereas the laws of the kingdom are spiritual laws. The world says work hard to earn money, whereas the kingdom law is, *give* and it shall be given to you. We *are* told to work hard in the kingdom, and laziness is condemned, but our Heavenly Father is the source of our income. I worked hard at being a dental surgeon, and likewise with my bookshop. Also in the church where I was a member. But my Heavenly Father was the source of my income. My dental practice made a profit, my bookshop work made a loss overall, and church work paid nothing (and often cost me money). But I worked hard at each, found tremendous fulfilment in them, and thanked the Lord for my income. These days I currently work at writing books and articles, I put many hours a week into a businessmen's fellowship, and I do work in the kingdom. Income comes from a variety of sources, and I thank my Heavenly Father for it. He is my supply.

Let's now stand a law of this world on its head, and suggest that if a child of God has insufficient income, perhaps they are not giving enough! Or perhaps they are not putting Jesus first.

I am probably being about as politically incorrect as one can get within the subject, not to mention being regarded as callous. But I am considering finance, money, income, spending, etc. within the context of the kingdom of God. I am considering finance within the context of Biblical teaching. And this is where the world and the true Church are poles apart. The world sees it as madness for someone struggling financially to put Jesus first, and give to him, his work and the poor before looking after themselves. Intelligent people would consider it irresponsible. But is this not what the Bible teaches about the kingdom?

And having written the above, how easy to then do the right thing for the wrong motive. To give, in order to get, does not work. To give, because the Bible says so, is also not the answer. We give as an expression of love and gratitude. We give because of relationship.

When I came to know Wendy, I really appreciated her lovely personality. She was just so kind. She did not have a large income, and she lived relatively simply, was quietly busy about the church, was devoted to her family, and was often entertaining people in her home. I came to love her, and married her. I had been through a challenging time financially (I had been plundered), but I was in a position to give to her. And that I did, whenever I could. Because I loved her. Still do. Always will. When we love someone, we do all we can to please them. And so we come to the question that is really at the heart of the issue - do I really love Jesus? And if I do, what priority do I give him?

Spending.

I have given a lot of space above to the subject of giving. But generally, as Christians, and in common with the world, we have little problem spending; saving can be neglected, but giving as a priority is the real issue.

Earlier in this chapter, I wrote that Christians can have varying, but strongly held views, on giving. The same applies to spending. There are those who believe that we should spend only on essential items, and give everything else to the Lord. Historically, John Wesley lived in that manner, and he was not alone in that. At the other end of the spectrum are those whose critics dub them the prosperity cult. New expensive cars (my current car is expensive - but quite old!), expensive homes, expensive toys... in fact, everything they have is expensive and luxurious. Unfortunately, those who subscribe to these widely differing lifestyles tend to teach that all true Christians should do likewise. The first group feel that everything should be given to God, whereas the second group believe that God is giving everything to his children to be enjoyed by them, and as a testimony to who he is. Both are easy to criticise. Both can appeal to our baser human nature, though in widely different ways, of course.

I do not find clear definitive *detailed* teaching in the Bible on how we should spend our money. In Bible times, most people had little money to spend, and so it was not the issue it is for Christians today. My own approach to this subject might seem a little unusual, but this is what I have found most helpful. I am created in the image of God. Like him, I have children. When I have given them money, what have I wanted them to do with it?

My four daughters have a lot in common, and have similar personalities and values in many respects. However, they are also very different from one another. When they were quite young, I started a savings scheme for each, putting in a small sum of money monthly over many years. As young ladies, each had a significant sum of money given to them. Not enough for a house, but a decent sum. What did I expect them to do with it? Firstly, I was tremendously moved by the letters I received from each of them. They showed such gratitude.

I wanted to cry, because I was so stirred. I think they realised the cost, as a relatively short time after starting the schemes, my first marriage ended and I was working hard and exercising serious faith in order to keep body and soul together. The savings schemes were for many years something of a burden. But a delightful burden, because I love my daughters.

Secondly, I expected each of them to use the money differently. They were different people at different stages of life. One might be buying a house, and putting it into that, whereas another could use it to help enjoy life at University, whilst another might invest it to grow for when the need arose. I would be surprised if each of them did not give some of it to the Lord's work in one way or another. The point is, my daughters are different people living different lives.

Thirdly, I did not expect any of them to waste the money. I am sure they did not.

In similar manner, I believe our Heavenly Father gives to us, knowing that we are different people living different lives. I think he expects each of us to put Jesus first. Unlike some Christians I have met, I believe our Father rather likes to see his children enjoying what he has given to them. I also believe that he does not want us to waste what he gives us.

A man I know received an inheritance, and for the first time in his life had some money to his name. With a Christian friend of similar disposition, they set up an ill-advised, poorly run business. It was only months before the money was gone and, once more, they were both struggling to live. What would their benefactor have thought? Was there not some responsibility to use the money to better their lives, and maybe others too? Our Heavenly Father is the Benefactor *par excellence!* Let us use his gifts to us responsibly. Let us never waste them. And let us never be selfish with them.

We recently gave a small sum of money to each of our grandchildren. (There are times when we feel that life would be simpler with less than nineteen of them, but they are each so delightful, and we love them to bits). Lovely handwritten letters were soon arriving in the post, and in addition to thanking us, one grandson had a question addressed to me. 'What shall I do with the money? What advice do you have for me, Grandpa?' I spent some time considering my answer, and then wrote to him, telling him that when I receive money, I thank God and give at least a little towards his work in this world. Then I consider. If there is something big that I have been wanting, I will either buy it, or put the money towards it. If there is nothing big that I want, I save the money until there is something, or some other need. But I do not save all of it, but use at least a little to enjoy myself. Some little treat.

I believe that because I am created in the image of God, I have, as a father, similar values and expectations as he has. And so when he gives me money, I think of my own children, and as a result, I give, spend and save.

Borrowing.

We live in an age when it is considered normal to borrow money for a variety of unnecessary items, and to live on credit. Our God speaks about borrowing and of being in debt, and we do well to pay heed to what he says.

He tells Israel that if they are faithful to him, he will bless them in many specific ways. One of these promises is *'You will lend to many nations but borrow from none. You will rule over many nations, but none will rule over you'*, Deuteronomy 15:6. There are a few things we can learn from this scripture.

Firstly, if Israel are faithful to the Lord, they will not be in a position where they need to borrow. In fact, the Lord will prosper them to the extent that they will be in a position to lend to others. There is a principle here, and we can apply it today. Where we are faithful to the Lord, he will bless us, meeting our needs and prospering us to the extent that we have more than we need. In such a situation, why would someone want to borrow? The answer is that they *want* something that they cannot currently afford. This is usually a new car, or an upgraded television or some other gadget, a new mobile phone, or similar. But consider this – if the Lord has not given us the money for this, do we really need it? The clear answer is 'No', though one is tempted to try and justify the desire for the new acquisition, with "I really need a more reliable car", or "Other people's children can watch so many more channels on their televisions than ours can. And a store in town is offering such reasonable terms". And so on.

Secondly, why is one not in a position to be content with what one has? Paul said, *"I have learned, in whatsoever state I am, therewith to be content". Philippians 4:11.* There are times when we do need something for which we do not have sufficient funds, and maybe need to reach out in faith. But we need to be real, because there is a temptation to reach out for what we *want* when the Lord has not spoken to us. *'Faith comes by hearing'* (Romans 10:17), and if we have not heard the Lord tell us to reach out in faith, there will be no faith. It is then an exercise of the flesh. A living relationship with the Lord brings fulfilment that nothing else can. Without it, one will be unfulfilled and generally dissatisfied, and tempted to feel that the latest gadget, new car, holiday, etc. will bring the fulfilment that is clearly absent. It will not. Having a relationship with the Lord brings contentment that nothing else does. And the Lord is pleased to prosper those who enjoy him and his presence.

Thirdly, we read in the Bible that if one is in debt, then one is under the power of the creditor. Consider again Deuteronomy

15:6, where we read, '*You will rule over many nations, but none will rule over you*'. When Israel were faithful to the Lord, they were ruling in life. They were in victory. To use a metaphor from Deuteronomy 28:13, they would be the head and not the tail. But the converse is true of those who are unfaithful to the Lord, and particularly where borrowing and debt is involved. The creditor has power over the debtor, who becomes the tail and not the head. People are evicted from their homes because they cannot pay the mortgage or the rent. The creditor has the power, and 'rules over the debtor'. Possessions can be repossessed where payments on debts and credit are not met. Another scripture tells us, '*The borrower is slave to the lender*', *Proverbs 22:7*. By following God's word, we can be the head and not the tail. By being faithful to the Lord, we can find that we are the ones who lend to others, and not those who find themselves under the power of others.

What I have written above borders on being politically incorrect at a time in history when it is considered normal to borrow in order to acquire luxuries that are really unnecessary. Luxuries are not wrong in themselves, but how does one get them? We live in an age and culture where people expect to have what they want now. Now! From instant coffee at all times of day, to instant sex when going out on a date, to instant new furniture when buying a home, to almost every gadget available under the sun. We are called to be *different*. We are called to live in such a relationship with the Lord that we experience contentment in daily life, enjoy the prosperity that he brings, and find ourselves living within our means and thanking the Lord for so many good gifts. A by-product of such living is good health, because one is thereby avoiding the stress that is rife in our materialistic credit-ridden society today.

'Owe no man anything, but to love one another', is a clear categorical, statement found in Romans 13:8. We do well to pay heed to teaching that is found consistently in both Old and New Testaments. Our Heavenly Father loves us and seeks to save us pain in this fallen world.

Paying Accounts.

During my professional life, I have attended many courses on *Practice Management* and similar subjects. Although not always advised by the lecturers, it was apparent that many businesses and professionals felt that they should withhold payment from creditors for as long as possible. This is bad practice for a Christian (or anyone else, in fact) for two reasons, one on principle, and the other pragmatic.

As soon as I receive goods or services, I am in debt to the provider. I owe them money. I have already stated that it is not Biblical to owe money, because this makes one a debtor, and under the power of the creditor. So - pay money you owe as soon as you can. In dental practice, it was standard accountancy to collect all invoices at the end of the month, and settle the statements (total of invoices from each company) at the end of the following month. However, the people of God are different - we settle our accounts as soon as possible. We do not owe people money.

Secondly, withholding monies owed can be bad practice from a pragmatic perspective. When I had equipment break down, and wanted an engineer as fast as possible, I would often be told, "We will give you priority. You pay your bills quickly". Similarly today when I need repair work carried out on our home, or similar, I have found that tradesmen are pleased to do business with me because they are paid as soon as they ask me, and ideally, as soon as they have finished their work.

So - pay your accounts promptly, and avoid being a debtor.

Saving.

After we have given to the Lord, his work and the poor, and when we have spent on necessities and other things, there is usually some more. There are times when there is not, and I have been there. I was there for five years as a student, and for quite some time after that. Also during the plundering years of divorce. But most people have times when money can be saved for the future, and the reason many people do not is that 'necessities' for them has a very broad definition!

Should we save at all? Once again, there are widely differing views on this subject amongst Bible-believing Christians. Some feel they should never save, but always be looking in faith to God. They quote scriptures that encourage faith, and speak of the Lord's care and provision for his children. At the other end of the spectrum are those who have a multitude of savings schemes, pensions, insurance policies and suchlike. These Christians will quote scriptures about us having a responsibility towards our families, and the biblical exhortations to be prudent. I have no problem with either of these views, unless those who hold them become legalistic and try to coerce others into doing what they do.

I have said above that the Bible has scriptures that point to having faith in God and to God's provision for us. There is also teaching on our responsibility towards our families, and that we should be prudent. I believe that extremes are to be avoided, if we are to respect *all* the scriptures. But we each need to be honest before God and seek to know his way for us. I find this beautifully illustrated in the lives of two friends of mine, a husband and wife. Paul and Mary (not their real names) are radically different from each other in so many ways. Paul felt called to mission work that brought in little, if any, income. That was certainly the case when he was younger, and probably not much different today. He always seems totally relaxed about this, though he does not take his faith lightly. He also works hard. Mary's way is about as different as you can get from Paul's. She too has worked hard, but policies and pensions have been very much a part of her lifestyle. They both live by faith, looking to the Lord to provide for them, both now and in the future. They both have scriptures that have led them in their respective ways of handling finance. They each respect the other's position. It works.

* * * * *

My financial advisor put his coffee down, smiled across the table and said, "Of course, you're my most successful client, Barrie".

There had been years when I had virtually nothing to save, and financial advisors simply helped me choose car insurance, home insurance and suchlike. However, finance had always interested me, and for years I had read the 'money' and 'business' sections of the newspapers. Then there had been the good years - after which it was all taken from me.

Lean years followed, though every need was met, and I always had 'more'. Putting the Lord first, giving, and looking after my family has always, I trust, been my priority. But it was part of my routine to save, even if it was tiny amounts. Coins went into a money box, and when there were enough for a banknote, they were exchanged for one and that was placed on one side. When there were enough banknotes to buy a National Savings certificate, I did so. Why a National Savings certificate? - because it was very safe and secure, and because one lost the interest if cashing it in early. That way, there was a big disincentive to spend it! After a few years, money from cashing in these certificates was placed in other safe investments.

Although I was seriously plundered at the age of fifty-seven, a small amount was retained. It was declared to the plunderers, but it was deemed to remain mine. Then, over the following years, it was as though the Lord did a 'loaves and fishes' operation on those investments, enabling me today to give, spend and save at a significantly higher level. I have been humbled by his generosity to such an undeserving person as myself, and try, by the grace of God, to be a good steward.

"And so what advice do *you* have for *me*?" asked my financial advisor. "What are the markets going to do next?"

(Take careful note - the Lord's way for me is unlikely to be his way for you. Be real with God about his financial direction in your life. I am sharing Biblical principles that all should follow, but we each need to know the Lord's individual application for us).

What is the Lord's way for you with regard to saving? You need to know, and if you have family responsibilities, you need to consider these things. We are created in the image of God - a Father who cares for and takes complete responsibility for his children, whilst teaching them each to exercise responsibility in their own lives. If created in his image, we should do likewise.

* * * * *

To summarise – the culture of the kingdom of God is very different from the culture of the world in which we live. Our values and priorities should be different from those of the world. If not, we need to evaluate why. Do we really love Jesus? Do we have an attitude of gratitude, and if so, how is that expressed?

Throughout the Bible, God's people are told to put him first. With regard to our money, giving to the Lord, his work, his people and the poor should be a priority. One reason we can fall short in this area is that we have adopted the culture, values and priorities of the world. We can regard as 'necessities' and 'rights' those *things* which are neither necessities nor rights.

For some Christians, saving is a low priority, especially if they do not have family responsibilities. Others are persuaded otherwise, and make provision for the future and in case of unforeseen times of need. Savings can also be used to yield significant additional income, which can enable enhanced giving.

Are you clear about what the Lord has laid on your heart? Then do not try and impose your particular ways and understanding on others; and do not let others coerce you into handling your money their way. We each need to be persuaded by the Lord, and we each need to be at peace. Because the Lord has made many promises with regard to these things, we can be assured that as we live with kingdom culture, we shall never be in need. We shall have success and prosperity.

Are you familiar with what the word of God teaches concerning money? Do you really realise what Jesus has done for you? Do you have an attitude of gratitude? If you have never done so, perhaps now is the time to consider these things. One thing you will find in the Bible is that it is the Lord's will that his children prosper. Let us continue to explore other aspects of coming into Biblical prosperity.

* * * * *

The Bible says, *'So then each one of us will give an account of himself to God'. Romans 14:12.*

Chapter 11

Generosity

Mark (not his real name) looked both embarrassed and excited as he walked over to me in church one Sunday. I was 'the director of finance', though any other church would have called me the treasurer. He explained that he and his wife felt they should give 10% of their income to the Lord, but were in a position to give only 2%. Mortgage, children's clothes, groceries, etc. were a necessary but too great a commitment. Their way of handling this was to 'do a deal with the Lord', Mark told me. The deal was that every time he received a pay rise, he would give 50% to the Lord, until he was giving 20% of his overall pay. This made me think of Jacob doing a deal with God at Bethel in Genesis 28:22.

Less than six weeks later, Mark walked over to me in church again, this time with the widest, silliest grin - he had received a pay rise. A big one. A few weeks later he was grinning again - another pay rise. Without exaggeration, I should think Mark came to me every two months or so during the following year, reporting pay rise after pay rise, and significantly bumping up his giving to the church. He summed up his experience by saying, "We've never given so much, and we've never had so much money left". Mark was learning generosity, and in turn experiencing the generosity of his Heavenly Father towards him and his family.

* * * * *

If there is one overriding message in the Sermon on the Mount of Matthew chapters 5, 6 and 7, it is that we are to be like our Father in heaven. With regard to giving, he is *generous*. Our God gives richly. For example, there is more than sufficient food in this world to feed every mouth, and so many more. (Let us not blame God for problems that are rooted in man's selfishness). He has made so many promises to his people concerning meeting needs, and more. Our God keeps his word. He is generous, and he calls us to be like him. Not that we are simply to 'do what the Bible says' in the area of giving, but that our nature should be like his - to give. We are not under law, but under grace. Giving because one has to is law; giving because one wants to is grace.

There are so many verses in Scripture about being generous, many in the book of Proverbs. Some are expressed in allegorical form.

'One gives freely, yet grows all the richer; another withholds what he should give, and only suffers want'. Proverbs 11:24.

'A generous person will prosper; whoever refreshes others will be refreshed'. Proverbs 11:25.

'Whoever is generous to the poor lends to the LORD, and he will repay him for his deed'. Proverbs 19:17.

'The generous shall themselves be blessed, for they share their food with the poor'. Proverbs 22:9.

The above verses not only commend generosity, but speak of the person practising it receiving more. Luke 6:38 tells us that giving is rewarded by receiving. Once again, we need to remind ourselves that each verse of Scripture needs to be placed within the context of the rest of the Bible. To take scriptures such as these, and then give money with the motive of receiving more back, is to miss the point; generosity should flow from a generous, godly heart, not a selfish one. But the straightforward statements of Scripture concerning generosity, along with the promises, make it quite clear that generous people will never be in need. The Lord says that the person who gives will receive back *good measure, pressed down, shaken together and running over* (Luke 6:38). That is speaking of abundance. That is speaking of prosperity. And let us not limit either what the Lord can do, or how he will do it. Mark, who I mentioned at the opening of this chapter, received an abundance through pay rises and bonuses from his work. Others I have known have received significant payments from policies they did not realise they had, or through inheritance, or gifts. There are so many ways in which the Lord can really bless the generous, and it is his nature to do so.

There are also many *examples* of generosity in the Bible. In Exodus 36:1-7 the people gave more than they were asked to give, and Moses had to tell them to stop. That is generosity! We can learn from this example and give more than we are asked for at times. In Genesis 45, we find Joseph being generous to his brothers and family, even though this would seem illogical in terms of worldly values; they had been worse than mean to him. Here is another example to challenge us. In Luke 10:25-37, the Good Samaritan gives more than money; he shows warmth, friendship, love, protection, etc. We are to be generous with money, but also with time, friendship, etc. In 2 Chronicles 31 we have the story of the people bringing in tithes for the reforms and restoration of temple worship during the reign of Hezekiah. We read that the people tithed 'abundantly'.

In 2 Corinthians 8:1-5 there is the well known passage where Paul speaks of the Macedonians overflowing generosity to those in need, even when they themselves were experiencing a time of poverty.

The outstanding example in the Bible is God himself. He so loved the world that he gave his Son (John 3:16). And then we read of Jesus himself, 'though he was rich, yet for your sake he became poor, so that you, through his poverty, might become rich' (2 Corinthians 8:9). And he is our example. He is the one we follow.

* * * * *

In the chapter on God's purpose in prospering his people, I have given several examples concerning generosity. Within the Church, I am continually coming across examples of the generosity of God's people. Sometimes it is in giving to those in need abroad during times of famine, or following disasters such as earthquakes or floods, etc. whilst it is often in personal acts of kindness to someone who needs financial help or encouragement. Building projects can be a drain on people's resources, but where they are focused on expanding the work of the church in helping the poor, it is amazing how generous people can be. There is also a 'by-product' of generosity - testimony of the blessing received from the Lord by those who give. Mark, whose story I briefly outlined at the head of this chapter, kept receiving pay rises. These blessed him; they made him happy, and he had a wide, silly grin. God was good to him, and in turn he wanted to give *more* to the Lord out of gratitude. And then the Lord gave him still more, from which he gave the Lord more – and so on. This became part of Mark's testimony; he was able to tell others a real story of how the Lord had been good to him.

Generosity can be spontaneous, where one sees a need and responds with generosity. It can also be planned, such as Mark's 'deal with God'. Many people give to church and charities through bank direct debiting, and this is another area where generosity can be planned.

* * * * *

I had been a Christian for a few years before I heard teaching on tithing. Tithing is the practice of giving the Lord 10% of one's 'increase'. Wages and other income and gifts are generally included. By the time I came across this teaching, I had read the Bible from cover to cover several times, and also spent an average of three hours a night for eighteen months studying and making notes on every chapter. I could not understand the teaching, as I knew that tithing was an Old Testament practice, and was not taught in the New Testament. Since those days, I have had nearly fifty more years of Bible study, teaching, and generally seeking God on truth. I hope I understand more.

The people of Israel were commanded to bring a tithe (tenth) of their crops and increase in livestock to the priests each year (Leviticus 27:30 states it clearly, though it is expanded upon elsewhere). This was used to support the priests, and to help the poor amongst them, especially the widows, orphans and foreigners (Deuteronomy 26:12). Having said that, it is clear from the Bible, both the history books as well as the books of the prophets, that the people were not very faithful in doing so.

However, there are two examples recorded in Scripture of people tithing before the Law. Abraham gave 'one tenth of everything' to the priest Melchizedek in Genesis 14:20. The second example is Jacob who, whilst fleeing from Esau, promised the Lord that if he looked after him and brought him safely back, then he would give him one tenth of everything that the Lord gave him (Genesis 28:22). The significance of these passages is that they are accounts of God's people tithing to him *before the Law*; that is, they were not tithing 'under law'. Abraham tithed at least once; maybe more often, or maybe not, as Scripture does not say. Jacob promised that at a future time he would give a tenth of his income to God, if the Lord looked after him. Knowing Jacob's character from what I read in the Bible, I wonder if he did!

In the New Testament, there is no instruction to tithe. Jesus mentions the Pharisees tithing herbs whilst omitting the greater demands of the Law to love God and their neighbour (Matthew 23:23). In Hebrews 7, the writer alludes to Abraham tithing to Melchisedek, but this is nothing to do with teaching on Christian giving, but on Christ's priesthood. Those who believe the Lord desires Christians to tithe, would say the New Testament is silent on the subject because it is assumed. Those who do not believe Christians are required to tithe would say the New Testament is silent because tithing does not apply after Calvary.

People tend to hold strong views on the subject of tithing, whether they are for it or against it. Those who advocate tithing tend to emphasise putting the Lord first, the fact that *all* God's people were commanded to tithe under the Mosaic Law, and that Abraham and Jacob tithed before the Law, and therefore whilst not under law. I sense that many of those who tithe suspect that many of those who do not, give less than they do. I also suspect that they are right in their suspicions.

Those who do not believe that the Lord requires Christians to tithe also emphasise that we should put the Lord first in all things. They point out that tithing to support the poor under the Law is unnecessary today in western society as taxation and government social care covers this. There is no teaching whatsoever on tithing for Christians in the New Testament, but a lot of teaching on generosity. We are under grace and not law, but have a responsibility to give generously to God's work and the poor. Those who advocate generosity as opposed to tithing may suspect that those giving a tenth feel they have 'ticked a box', and are less willing to be generous when needs arise which are not covered by the tithe (tithes usually go to the minister/pastor's pay and regular upkeep of church buildings). They may also suspect that ministers and pastors feel more financially secure if they can persuade their congregations to give a tenth of their incomes into the offering.

I have tried to be fair with regard to advocates of both sides in the tithing debate, and would see my own position as follows.

Tithing is for Jews living under the Mosaic Law. Of course, they should not be under this Law because Christ has set them free. But if I was an Orthodox Jew today, I think I would see tithing as obligatory.

Tithing is for Christians who believe the Lord has told them to. Mark (above) came close to this position, and I have a number of Christian friends who believe the Lord has told them to do so.

Tithing is a temporary discipline for some Christians at some times. There was a time when I tithed, even though I was quite clear that Christians were not obliged to do so. I felt it was right for me at that time, and it helped me realise what meaningful giving entailed, as I had previously given much lesser amounts. Galatians 4:1-5 speaks of God's people being under the Law, which brought them to Christ. I believe Paul is alluding to the many types (pictures) of Christ within the Law, which led at least some of the Jews to recognise Christ and come into freedom. I would not want to push this too far, but discipline (not law) can lead us to liberty. Christians are to embrace and enjoy both discipline and liberty, whilst avoiding the extremes of bondage and licentiousness.

* * * * *

Basic New Testament teaching on giving is found in 1 Corinthians 16:2. Teaching on giving is obviously found throughout Scripture, but this verse does encapsulate much.

'On the first day of the week, let each one of you lay something aside, storing up as he may prosper, that there be no collections when I come'.

Priority. On the *first* day of the week. At the beginning of each week, Paul tells the Christians in Corinth to put aside money for the Lord's work and the poor. They are to give priority to this. So should we. We should not demonstrate the *Me! Me! Me!* society, but the *Jesus! Jesus! Jesus!* society. We don't just talk the talk, but walk the walk and put Jesus first.

Regularity. It is implied that Christians should do this *every* week. This can be seen as legalistic, but that depends on your heart. There may be exceptions to this, because we are *not* under law. But generally, we will be regularly giving to the Lord's work, his people and the poor.

Everyone. The verse says *each* of you. If you feel that giving is generally for 'them others', you need to examine your heart.

Proportionately. The Scripture says 'as he may prosper'. This means that those who receive a lot should give a lot. Those who receive little will give little. It's really quite simple and sensible. But as the Lord prospers us, we can give more, and receive more, and give more, and receive more… That's how it works (Luke 6:38).

* * * * *

I have written quite a lot on the subject of generosity, but let us return to look again at Jesus. Jesus is one expression of the Father's generosity to us (John 3:16). Jesus himself is wonderfully generous to us (2 Corinthians 8:9).

The Lord has given us so much revelation concerning himself - his love, kindness, mercy, grace, promises of provision and abundance and needs met, etc. - towards his people. He has given us so many promises of providing for us, sustaining us, giving to us lavishly, etc.

Is this revelation true? Are the promises in Scripture to be taken seriously? If so, how are we handling them? If we are handling them responsibly, are we experiencing the truth and reality of them? Are we prospering in a Biblical sense?

If these things are so, should generosity not flow from hearts that worship Jesus with both awe and love? If we are not prospering, perhaps we need to return to the teaching on who our Heavenly Father is, and on his promises, and allow the Spirit to speak them to us, creating faith in our hearts. Faith in a Father who will always meet our needs generously - and give more, so that we can give to him and those in need.

* * * * *

The Bible says, *'A generous person will prosper; whoever refreshes others will be refreshed'. Proverbs 11:25.*

Chapter 12

Sowing and Reaping

Friends of ours employed a nanny to look after their children. She lived in their home, where they fed her and gave her £15 a week, which was at that time worth considerably more than today. At a Christian meeting she attended, an offering was taken. She heard the Lord say to her, "Put in all of your week's pay". But that would leave nothing, she thought. Nothing for a whole week. But convinced that she was hearing God, she popped her pay, all of it, into the offering basket as it passed her.

After the meeting, the speaker was given a gift of £150 by the organisers. But he too heard the voice of the Lord. As he prepared to leave, he handed the gift he had received to the nanny's employer, saying "The Lord has told me to ask you to give this to your nanny".

* * * * * *

It was around the year 1980 when, totally unexpectedly, a bill for additional tax popped through my letter-box. Not only had I not anticipated such a demand, but it was for more than I had available to pay it at the time. It was big.

"How will you handle that?" enquired a full-time minister I was working with on a convention just then, and in whom I had confided about the bill.

I knew what to do, as I felt the Spirit had prompted and prepared me. "I must review my giving", I replied. "I believe the Lord is showing me that I should really be giving more at this time".

I include this story, as I feel it illustrates quite clearly how the laws of the kingdom are so very different from the laws of the world. In the world, the reaction would be 'give less, and spend less' in order to save the money to pay the taxman. It is not necessarily so within the kingdom of God, though it might be appropriate to review one's finances generally at such a time. The Bible says, "*Give*, and it will be given to you".

Perhaps it is needless to say that I reviewed my giving and acted as I felt directed. Also, the tax bill was paid on time.

* * * * *

As Jesus walked the roads and hillsides of Galilee and Judea, he would teach his followers about the kingdom of heaven. His teaching was engaging, which was one reason why crowds of people were drawn to him. His teaching was usually clear, though those not wanting to understand found it easy to do just that when parables were presented. And he would usually illustrate with objects that people did understand, to explain things that they had not previously grasped.

"Look at the birds. They do not worry about where their next meal will come from". "Look at the flowers. They are not anxious about being clothed". Sheep, coins, sunsets, sons, and other everyday objects, creatures, people and situations are used by Jesus to explain spiritual matters concerning the kingdom of God.

In the Bible, sowing and reaping is sometimes used to explain kingdom principles concerning giving and receiving. This applies generally, but especially with regard to finance, and is enlarged upon to some extent in 2 Corinthians 9:6-8. Paul was writing to Christians in Corinth, but this teaching has been preserved in the Scriptures for us today.

If we sow sparingly we shall also reap sparingly. Likewise, we are told that if we sow generously, we shall also reap generously. The application is general, and cannot be applied in a legalistic manner. Our God is bigger than we are, and our God is more generous than we are. He makes the sun to shine, and sends the rain, on both the righteous and unrighteous (Matthew 5:45). But the person who is mean and tight-fisted is unlikely to enjoy financial blessing from heaven, and the generous are unlikely to live in need.

However, the 'sowing and reaping' teaching is not confined to the teaching of Jesus, or indeed, to the New Testament. In Proverbs 11:24 we read, 'Give freely and become more wealthy'. There is both teaching and an assumption in this verse. Solomon is writing to those who were God's people of the Old Testament, Israel, and in particular, for those seeking wisdom and success (Proverbs 1:1-3). The teaching is that if you give freely, you will receive back. But it does not just say 'give', but 'give freely', which speaks of attitude. That is how our Father gives – freely. We are to be like him. It is possible to spend so long weighing up whether to give to a cause or a situation or a person, that the need has already been met by the time one decides to give. If you give freely, you don't spend too long thinking about it first, though one is expected to use prudence (common sense) and wisdom. The assumption is that one already has wealth. The person who gives freely becomes 'more wealthy' in this translation. And the assumption is therefore that the person has wealth to start with. This sits comfortably with verses such as 3 John 2, where the inspired writer wishes 'prosperity and health as one's soul prospers'.

Verses on sowing and reaping have been, at times, abused by some, and as a result misunderstood by others. Firstly, the verses have been used in a legalistic and manipulative manner by preachers seeking to fill their coffers from the pockets of those sitting under their 'ministry'. "Sow your seed, and you will reap a great harvest", is presented in such a manner that people believe that if they put money in the offering (which will go to the preacher), the Lord will reward them by giving a 'harvest' amounting to several times the amount they have 'sown'. I have also read this in literature sent out by evangelists and missionaries, and heard it taught on Christian television. It is certainly attractive, or perhaps seductive, to those who need more money, and I am sure it increases the size of the offering. Only a small minority of 'ministers' use this technique, though some are of high profile.

But our God does not want people to give cash because they believe they will get more back. The implication is that if you give £5, you can expect a much larger sum to come back to you. It is as though the Lord is a heavenly slot machine, and the teaching suggests that if you put more money in, more will come out. This is subtly different from the real meaning of the Bible, which is the word of God.

But before we come to the true teaching of these scriptures, let us consider a further problem resulting from this false teaching. What is the effect on the people giving if they do not receive more back?

Firstly, instead of becoming disillusioned with the preacher, they can become disillusioned with the Bible, or with God himself. Hence the situation I alluded to earlier, where a man I knew quite well stopped giving to the church because 'it doesn't work'. *What* did not work? *Who* had told him that if he tithed, he would receive more back? Unfortunately, giving and receiving had been presented as a mechanical cause and effect arrangement, and when that did not work, Brian (not his real name) felt disillusioned about giving to the Lord and his work.

Another potential problem is that the person will then give more than they really want to, and probably more than they can afford. And, of course, they will probably lose that too. Not only will disillusionment set in, but cynicism and perhaps poverty. In addition to the personal loss of faith and possible financial hardship, the preaching and its effects are a bad witness to a watching world.

The key to experiencing the truth of sowing and reaping lies in one's attitude, and in one's relationship with the Lord. In 2 Corinthians 9:8, we read, "God loves a cheerful giver". The actual Greek word translated *cheerful* is *hilarus*, from which the English word *hilarity* is derived. However, although hilarity would be a poor translation of *hilarus,* we can learn from this derivation. Hilarity is often associated with something extremely funny, maybe farcical. It can conjure up a picture of someone rolling on the floor, squealing with mirth. Whereas that is not what either Paul, who wrote the second letter to the Corinthian Christians, or the Holy Spirit, who inspired the letter meant, there is here more than a hint at the truly joyful nature of giving to someone you love.

So, if you don't have a loving relationship with the Lord, it is extremely unlikely that you will be a cheerful giver in the manner described. And this explains why coldly giving into a collection bag, or to a television evangelist, with the expectation that there will be a 'harvest of cash' flowing back to the giver, usually results in disappointment.

Consider - someone brings you a gift. There is no smile and no warmth, and more than a hint of the fact that they are doing what someone has told them to do. Maybe they would rather have kept the gift for themselves, had it not been for others exerting pressure. How do you feel? Does it bring you joy? Does it touch your heart? And maybe you then suspect that they are now waiting for you to reward them for what they have done?

But then imagine a different scenario, where you receive a gift that comes with warmth and a smile, from someone who loves you and wants to express that love. They want to bring you joy. Their heart is to bless you. They are not waiting to receive. It's not all about them - it's all about you.

In the second situation, we have the same donor, recipient and gift. But the heart attitude is totally different, and that changes everything. Where there is no relationship and no obvious affection, the response of the recipient is likely to be as cold as that of the giver. But where there is warmth, affection, love and gratitude, the recipient will be moved to respond in a meaningful manner.

Jesus has been so very good to me, and I thank him every day. I have a Heavenly Father who showers Wendy and me with blessings day after day. We pray together every morning, and invariably thank him, with a real sense of wonder at his kindness towards us. He has always looked after us, and yet we have each in the past found ourselves looking into a future where we believed all needs would be met - but not much more. Now, we can hardly believe the ways in which our Father has blessed us. In our praying, we thank him for our salvation, knowledge of his presence with us, protection, provision... home, clothes, holidays... and so undeserved. Of course we give. Cheerfully and thankfully. We want to. We delight to. Not sowing with a view to reaping. Just cheerfully giving to someone we love, as part of our 'Thank you Father'. Giving to those spreading the word and doing the work that will bring others into this heavenly family where all are blessed so richly. Giving to the underprivileged. Giving where we feel the Spirit's prompting.

Our Father continues to bless us. Richly. Abundantly. We are filled with joy and thankfulness, and guess how we express our gratitude!

* * * * *

Do you ever consider why God created us?

We read that 'God is love' (1 John 4:8). Such statements and eternal truths can easily be rolled out, yet in a meaningless manner. What does it mean that God is love? What does it tell us of the nature of God? If God was present before creation (and he was), how could he 'be love' in a meaningful way?

The truth lies in the fact of the Trinity. The Father eternally loves the Son and the Spirit. The Son pleases the Father. The Spirit honours the Son and pleases the Father. Eternally, love is expressed and flowing within the Godhead. For mortal man to seek to understand the Godhead is at best, 'looking through a glass darkly'. And yet there is such revelation in Scripture by the Spirit. Furthermore, we are told that we are created 'in the image of God' (Genesis 1:27). Husband and wife, ideally, love, honour and respect one another. Furthermore, they love their children. Love? They protect them, provide for them, train them and seek the best for them. This is no lucky accidental result of serendipitous and fortuitous chance happenings in an atheistic universe where the Second Law of Thermodynamics strongly suggests that *decay* is the prevalent process. Love in the ideal family is an expression of that family being 'in the image of God'. The love expressed towards children by parents is an expression of them being 'in the image of God'. And here we have more than a clue regarding the purpose of creation.

Our Heavenly Father desires a family within which love is freely expressed and received. And so creation. But love can only be expressed through free will, and that brings vulnerability to sin. Hence the big plan of salvation, where the Father reaches out to children who are both born into, and simultaneously adopted, into his family; children with free will who choose to trust in him. Children whose sin has been cleansed forever through the shed blood of Christ. And so the heavenly family expresses and receives love. The Father lovingly gives. We lovingly give. Sowing? Reaping? There is indeed such an aspect when seen in earthly terms. But the heart of the matter is love.

* * * * *

This brings us back to our friend's nanny at the beginning of the chapter. Within a loving relationship with her Heavenly Father, she felt the Holy Spirit urge her to give one whole week's pay, which was all that she had, to the Lord. For his work. Maybe she hesitated, to be sure of the leading. And then, with cheerfulness, she put her £15 into the offering. She had a loving Father. He always looked after her. All would be well.

I wonder if she later reflected on what had happened? Was it really the Holy Spirit? Would she manage? We indeed have an enemy who whispers negativity and doubts into our souls.

And then, perhaps a day or so later, she is handed an envelope. It comes from someone she heard speak, but does not know. With curiosity she opens the envelope. I will leave you to imagine her surprise, her elation, and her thankful heart.

She sowed. She reaped. It was a simple act of obedience to the leading of the Holy Spirit. It was probably lifestyle. It was training from on high. It was life as it is meant to be lived in the kingdom of God.

Jesus said, "Give, and it shall be given to you; good measure, pressed down, shaken together and running over will be poured into your lap. For with the measure you use, it will be measured to you". (Luke 6:38). The nanny's experience is such a clear example of this promise being fulfilled in the life of an ordinary Christian. But this is no isolated example. Read the life of George Muller. There are a number of biographies, and the miracles experienced as he gave himself to the Lord's work in looking after orphans is absolutely amazing. That was Bristol, UK in the 19th century. And today, in the UK and in all countries of the world, people are finding that the promises of our God recorded in the Bible, are just as relevant today as they always have been. They are not there for people to 'grab a promise, believe and receive', but for God's people to enjoy success and prosperity as they in turn give to that work of extending the kingdom and building the Church.

We are called primarily to a relationship of love with the Father and Son through the Spirit. Time alone with the Lord is probably his greatest desire for us. He loves to see us identifying with his family as we meet with church for praise, worship, fellowship and working together at extending the kingdom. And giving is a normal part of the life of a child of God.

Remember what our God teaches us through 2 Corinthians 9:6-8. Those who sow sparingly will reap sparingly. Those who sow lavishly will reap lavishly. But it flows from relationship and it flows from the heart, so invest in your relationship with Jesus. Spend time with him. Reflect on what he has done for you. Consider what he is doing for you. And from a truly thankful, cheerful praising heart, make lavish sowing a part of your everyday lifestyle.

* * * * *

The Bible says, '*Consider this: Whoever **sows sparingly** will also reap sparingly, and whoever sows generously will also reap generously. Each one should give what he has decided in his heart to give, not out of regret or compulsion. For God loves a cheerful giver*'. 2 Corinthians 9:6-8.

Chapter 13

Wisdom

A beggar stepped out of the shadows and held a bowl in front of me. I ignored it, but Mike (not his real name) stopped, took out some coins, and placed them in the bowl.

"We must always remember what the good Lord told us, Barrie". he said, gently rebuking me. "Give to everyone who asks you", he added, quoting the words of Jesus from Luke 6:30.

Suddenly, a further fifteen or so beggars emerged from the shadowed recesses in the bridge, holding out bowls and clearly converging on Mike. "Oh heck!" he gasped, and took to his heels!

* * * * *

I was visiting my daughter Naomi in Mostar. She had been there a few years, working amongst people whose lives had been traumatised, often devastated, by the most recent of the Balkan wars. I loved those times, as she showed me round East Mostar in particular, with its medieval architecture and numerous alleys, where artisans displayed their merchandise for the passing tourists. Except there were few tourists in those days, with the iconic *Stari Most* (literally 'old bridge') destroyed in the war, and the main shopping boulevard reduced to two rows of battle-scarred burnt-out ruins. But there were beggars.

Mike and his wife arrived from the UK, considering whether to apply to join the mission that my daughter worked with. They rested for an hour or two, to recover from one of the longest and roughest bus rides of their life. Maybe it was only around 100 miles, but it could feel like 1,000 on a Balkan bus. I did not know Mostar like my daughter, but she suggested I take Mike for a walk by the river Neretva, to give him a taste of the place. We came to the bridge constructed to temporarily replace the *Stari Most*, until a new permanent replica of the original was complete. It was dusk, and as we stepped onto the structure, the first beggar emerged from the shadows. Two minutes later, Mike was running for his life!

So, was Mike correct in his initial application of Luke 6:30, or was his revised reaction to the beggars' requests the better way? I am sure that mature Christians would probably be split on that question, and sometimes every way seems wrong. Certainly, Satan will whisper in our ear that we have been wrong, whichever line of action we take.

Every verse of Scripture needs to be read and evaluated within the context of the whole. We are told to give to everyone who asks us, and yet if we did that, literally, we could soon be cleaned out financially, whilst the cash we had given might well, in part, be used for drug abuse and similar. But then again, we can use such an argument as an excuse for not giving to the needy, when Jesus would.

Throughout the Scriptures, we are told to show practical care for the poor. Widows and orphans are mentioned, as these were people who were low in assets, and with very little opportunity to work. They were truly needy, and God's people were encouraged to give to them. The principle found there can be applied today.

Another principle stated throughout Scriptures, is to have and to use wisdom. The book of Proverbs is saturated with the subject of wisdom. However, there are many New Testament passages too, where we are exhorted to have wisdom.

In 1 Timothy 5:3 we are told to support widows. The expression used is 'widows indeed'. The implication is that if a widow asks Christians to support her financially, they are to discern first whether she is a 'widow indeed'. This tells us that Luke 6:30 is not to have a blanket application. Wisdom is required. The following verses, 1 Timothy 5:4-7, indicate *how* wisdom is to be applied. If the widow has family who can support her, she is not to be a burden to the church.

One of the gifts of the Holy Spirit listed in 1 Corinthians 12:8-10 is the discerning of spirits (verse 10). *Why* is a person begging? For *what* will they use money given to them? And this does not just apply to beggars, but to others who might ask for your money, including charities (how much really goes to the charity?), television evangelists (are they self-indulgent with money given them?), or the person who tells you how they have been cheated by others (have they really? have you heard both sides of their story?) resulting in them being virtually destitute (are they really?). Very regularly, Christians and ministers and evangelists and apostles in Asia and especially, Africa, ask me for money and support over the Internet. Most of them are completely unknown to me. And having said that, I am sure that some are genuine, and I have on rare occasions, sent money out to a needy person. I hope I have rightly used wisdom and discernment. The innocent naivety of giving to every good cause and to everyone who asks may be childlike, but discernment comes with maturity.

A couple I know have a son who for many years has been addicted to almost any drug he can lay his hands on. He goes to treatment centres, but usually walks out before the process has started. His parents have housed him, and given him an incalculable amount of cash over many years. Of course they want to help him, but now they are impoverished and their son is no better. Have they used discernment? Sometimes even the soft option is hard, but the more difficult way is right.

The brother of a friend was co-ordinating the visit of a world famous evangelist to a city in the UK. Although an ardent 'fan' of the man, even he was shocked to be told that the evangelist *had* to stay in the penthouse flat at the best hotel ('This is not negotiable'), and *had* to have fresh apples daily from a certain country ('This is not negotiable'), and *had* to have fresh peaches daily from another country ('This is not negotiable') and so on down a seemingly endless list. How can Christians mindlessly revere such a man, and give large sums of money to his 'ministry'. Curiously, many people are saved through that man, and miracles happen. But his demanding self-indulgence disqualifies him from such donations, in my eyes, whilst I praise God for every soul saved and every body healed.

We are exhorted to give financially to the poor, the underprivileged, those caught up in wars, famines, disasters, earthquakes, etc. We are called to be generous. We are called to be lavish with our giving. But we are also called to be discerning.

Some years ago, we were returning from an Indian restaurant where we had enjoyed dinner with a Christian couple with whom we were friends. Walking through the city centre, a beggar sitting on the pavement looked up and said, "I'm hungry. Please help". Beside him was a bowl where passers-by could deposit coins. Stephanie's hand dived into her bag, and she produced an object wrapped in paper. Handing it to the beggar, she said, "Eat this". As we continued on our journey, I enquired what was in the paper. "A naan bread", she replied. "I bought it in the restaurant, and was taking it home for my dogs. His need is greater". Wisdom, and the Lord having prepared her for the situation. Money could have been abused. Ignoring him could have been wrong. But my wife tells me that one naan bread has sufficient calories for one man for one day.

Some of what I have written above can be used as an excuse for ignoring the plight of those in need, but that is a greater wrong than giving to those who really do not need the money. Always remember Jesus' interpretation of the Old Testament law – 1. put God first, 2. people are more important than things, and 3. needs are more important than rights. But use kingdom money efficiently by using wisdom and discernment.

* * * * *

Wisdom is also important in decisions concerning aspects of life related to the *receiving* of finance. 'For I know the plans I have for you, declares the Lord, plans for welfare and not for evil, to give you a future and a hope', says Jeremiah 29:11. I have stated earlier that all verses of Scripture need to be considered within the context of the whole Bible, and this verse flows very much with the rest of Scripture. The immediate context of the verse just quoted is the captivity of the people of Judah in Babylon, but two principles are clearly seen here. Firstly, the Lord has a plan for his people, and secondly, his plan is the best way forward. However, we need to use wisdom in discerning the Lord's plan for us, as there are usually temptations to go in other directions, as well as distractions along the way.

In choosing a career, financial reward can be a significant temptation. I had one dentist work for me who had a photograph of a Porsche on his surgery wall. "That's my aim in life", he told me with a grin. Maybe it was, but he was never going to own one unless he changed his attitude to his work and his patients. He was not a believer, and I suspect that it was the envisioned lifestyle that influenced his career choice. There is nothing wrong with owning a Porsche, or in wanting to have such a car, but a child of God needs to know the Father's direction. I have at times had one or two powerful cars, and also one or two bangers along the way. But this dentist had little real interest in caring for people, and with my encouragement, left my city practice very quickly – faster than a Porsche.

I was well into my university course when I came to faith in Christ, and so the direction of my life had to some degree, been decided. I did consider whether I should continue with dentistry, as the life I came to experience as a Christian was a dramatic change from anything I had known before, and I felt maybe I should be full-time in helping others come into the kingdom. But there was no clear leading to do so, and I continued with my dental studies.

Within the world of dentistry, there are a number of options regarding the nature of one's career. I had always wanted to be a family dentist with a High Street practice, and I felt no desire whatsoever to work in a hospital or community service. I did become aware of the need for missionary work, and considered going to Asia to work on a mission as a dentist. My wife and I prayed, and waited. There seemed no word from heaven, and so we stayed in the UK.

Chasing money can lead to frustration. Seeking the will of God and his wisdom is the way that brings fulfilment – and prosperity is promised for those who are faithful. Needs met, and more. For some a little more, and for others, so much more. But always more. Seeking God led me to work in Dorset, where I had a modest income and found life was so good. Five years later saw us moving to Norfolk, as we were clearly led to do so. We did not expect a large income, but we did expect fulfilment – and the Lord gave us both in abundance. But seek wisdom, seek the will of God, and follow Jesus.

Following a career because of financial reward, or chasing a life-partner because they are attractive, can seem to offer so much. But wisdom from heaven alone leads to fulfilment and prosperity in this life, and a life to look forward to in the world that is to come.

Seek wisdom!

* * * * *

The Bible says, *'If any of you lacks wisdom, you should ask God, who gives generously to all without finding fault, and it will be given you'. James 1:5*

Chapter 14

Work

Stuart and I were members of the same church. He worked on a farm. One year he planted potatoes, and looked after them until harvest time. He was then told that because of regulations associated with the European Union, he was not to harvest the potatoes, but to plough them back into the ground. He did not lose financially from it, but was deeply disappointed. We are called to work productively, and without that, we are unfulfilled.

* * * * *

Frank wanted to be an architect. His father was a station master on the Great Northern Railway, and was often getting promotions. In fact, friends said that one day he would probably be station master at the prestigious Kings Cross station in London. And then, Frank's father stepped in front of a train. Not only did Frank's father die, but so did Frank's hopes of being an architect.

He needed to become a bread winner for the family, and quickly. He secured a job as a clerical worker on the railway, and supported his mother and family. Later he married, and had a family of his own. He worked on the railway until he retired, and then looked after his garden, read the newspaper, watched television - and became incredibly bored. So he looked for something to do, and started working part-time for a local engineering company. He found the work fulfilling

- and he was paid. As well as his railway pension. And the garden, newspaper, and television.

Frank was still working in his seventies, and enjoying it. That is what we are designed to do - work. And he was better off financially. I remember Frank - as a fulfilled, contented man, and a much-loved grandfather. Mine!

* * * * *

I have known Kevin for many years. He associates loosely with churches. He has never worked, though I am not sure why. His health appears good, though it is off limits for discussion. He spends most of his time playing games on his computer, and is financed through government benefits. Life is boring, and he gets very drunk at times. Occasionally the police take him away for a night or two. One day Kevin met Tracey, over the Internet. She moved in with him. They play computer games. The government gives them money. Life is boring. They both get drunk.

We are designed to work productively. Without doing so, we are unfulfilled.

* * * * *

John was a successful businessman – until a creditor failed to pay his company. John went bankrupt, had a heart attack that left him in a wheelchair, and then his wife left him. At a Christian meeting, John asked for the laying on of hands and prayer, and then stood up from his wheelchair, and walked again. He stored the wheelchair back at home in a cupboard.

John is not wealthy in the eyes of the world, and by its values. He is not young, but he prospers. Every need is met, and he has more. When I first became acquainted with John, he was cooking lunches for his friends and neighbours, and anyone else who called in. No-one was charged. Several Italian dishes, or on another occasion, a variety of curries and rices, were the result of his labours. His home is not large, and people would hand plates in through the front door, and go home with a stack of food. I sat in the wheelchair – there was nowhere else to sit.

Until recently, John has visited a supermarket at the end of the day when their 'best before' dates are nearing expiry. He buys food at bargain prices, and distributes to those who really need them. Rather than do nothing, John has worked creatively and industriously, being a real blessing to his friends and neighbours. I know few people, if any, who are more contented or more fulfilled, than John. In the eyes of the world, he has very little. But God gives him 'more' and he works with it, productively, and blesses others as well as leading a fulfilled life.

* * * * *

We are told to work! That is not a popular thing to say, especially as we live in an age when the emphasis seems to be on leisure and entertainment. But in the Bible we are told to work.

God himself is seen as a worker, firstly in Genesis 1:1-15. For six days he worked, and then for one day he rested. We are made in the image of God. If work was not good, God would not have done it. Work *is* good. But God's work is productive, and when he looks at the result, he sees that it is good. That brings a sense of fulfilment (Genesis 1:31). Created in the image of God, we are called to productive work, which will bring us fulfilment.

There is a society in the UK which promotes Sunday as being a day of rest. They used to be fairly high profile within Christian and secular society. Because our culture is now so strongly secular, they are rarely reported in the press. The scripture they quoted most was Exodus 20:9 - 'Six days you shall labour and do all your work, but the seventh is a Sabbath to the LORD your God'. The emphasis of this society was that people should not work on Sunday; that it should as far as possible, be a day of rest. But did this focus overlook the fact that the seventh day in Old Testament times was Saturday and not Sunday? More importantly, the six days of work received little mention compared with the one day of rest.

The above scripture did not just command those living under the Old Testament law to rest on Saturday (strictly speaking, from sunset Friday to sunset Saturday), but it also told them to work on the six preceding days. Those who were unable to work through infirmity of one form or another ('the poor'), were to be cared for by the community. The people were not to totally glean their vineyards (Leviticus 19:10) or harvest their grain fields into the corners (Leviticus 23:22). The 'poor' could gather freely in those places. The people of Israel were told to be open-handed towards those who had fallen on hard times (Deuteronomy 15:7-8, 9-10). However, these scriptures do not negate the commandment to 'work six days and rest one' found in the Ten Commandments of Exodus 20.

The Church is not under law - it is under grace. However, there are two relevant considerations concerning this Old Testament commandment. Firstly, the commandment was given for the good of God's people, and so the principle stands: working six days and resting one is good for us. Maybe not rigidly applied, and certainly not legalistically, but in general terms. Secondly, those who are grateful for the salvation they enjoy, will want to please the Lord. Working pleases the Lord, as does resting in order to focus more on him.

The Lord loves the poor, and has always been concerned for them. Today, western societies have social care systems that care for the under-privileged. Indeed, these societies are based largely on Christian and Biblical principles and make provision for the sick, the handicapped, the poor, et al. Many other cultures in the world do not.

The New Testament also flows with this 'working and resting' principle, and states it in a manner that some members of western society might well find politically incorrect, if not downright offensive. 'The one who is unwilling to work shall not eat,' (2 Thessalonians 3:10). The person who was able-bodied and did not work, would not be given help. Those who are physically or mentally unable to work should be looked after, not least by the State through our taxation system. Churches can supplement this where appropriate, and especially where the person is acting responsibly, or will receive help in learning appropriate behaviour. The problem is those who are unwilling to work, and who are content to receive money which, in effect, comes from the taxed incomes of those who *are* working. To effectively police the system in order to make sure it is not abused is too expensive.

We are called to work, and to do so in a manner whereby we do not need to look to the State. We are to be responsible for ourselves There are times of sickness and incapacity, and indeed old age frailty, when people might need to draw from the State into which some of their past earnings have been paid as tax. But Christians look to the Lord – and, if possible, they work. Some time ago, I was looking at the benefits of our social security system in the UK, and said to a close friend, "It really is a wonderful system. If it was not for social security benefits, a number of our friends would be dead". The response was immediate, as my companion said, "Not true. If it was not for social security benefits, a number of our friends would be *working*". That statement is wildly politically incorrect, and there are those who would object strongly and vocally. But the Bible, God's word, says the same, 'The one who is unwilling to work shall not eat'.

We look to the Lord to supply all that we need, including our income. But we have a responsibility to work. As a University student, I worked hard, often until 2 a.m. having started at 9 a.m. I qualified, and worked in dental practice. Later I had a Christian bookshop. For a number of years I spent one day a week driving from my practice to the homes of housebound, chronically sick, and usually elderly, poor people in order to treat them dentally, often making them false teeth. They had no money to pay me, and the National Health Service fees did not cover my expenses. But it was work that was productive and fulfilling. I retired from dental practice in 2007, but since then have spent many hours every week writing, speaking, organising Christian businessmen's meetings, and working in the church. With regard to income, the Lord looks after me. The work I carry out is productive and fulfilling, though not everything I do carries a payment as such.

We are called to work. Let us do so. Not only is this pleasing to the Lord, but it is fulfilling for us. We need to use prudence, and we need to use wisdom. Although we look to the Lord as our supply, some work brings far greater financial rewards than others. We need to be aware of this, and prayerfully use wisdom. But the financial reward is not the decisive factor in determining what work we do. Some of my dental work was very rewarding financially, and I could have engaged in that exclusively. Visiting patients in their homes cost *me*! But it was productive and worthwhile, benefited the people treated, and was not carried out by many of my colleagues. The bookshop made a profit some years, but generally did not. It made a significant overall loss. If making money had been my primary aim, my working week would have been much different.

We are called to work - work that brings in an adequate income, work that is productive, and work that is fulfilling. Laziness has no place in the Christian life. A person once came to our church, and a few weeks later we visited him in his home. He was usually in. He tapped away at his laptop, and there were used coffee mugs around. He sounded very spiritual, but it was difficult to understand what he actually did for a living. Then a lady in our fellowship mentioned him. He had once worked briefly under her management, though he had not recognised her when he visited our church. "One day was enough", she said. "He was so *lazy*. I told the agency not to send him again. I would never have guessed that he was a Christian". We suspected that he lived largely on government benefits, though he was physically and mentally well. He was at our church a relatively short time, and in and out of other fellowships once he had left ours..

Our Heavenly Father has promised to look after his children. However, we have certain responsibilities, most of which I try to cover in these chapters. One of them is to work - productively. As we do so, the Lord will provide, and indeed prosper us.

* * * * *

The Bible says: *'Six days you shall labour and do all your work'. Exodus 20:9.*

'If a man will not work, he shall not eat'. 2 Thessalonians 3:10.

Chapter 15

Forgive Us Our Debts

Andy and Gail were new patients - and they were Christians. They needed to return to the surgery for two further appointments, and we enjoyed sharing some of our experiences of the Lord together. I completed the fillings, and scaling and polishing their teeth. They were good people. Until they did not pay their bill. Three accounts were sent at monthly intervals, and then a letter asking if there was a problem with my treatment, which went unanswered. They lived around fifteen miles out of the city, but I decided to bite the bullet and drive out to see them.

I rang the doorbell, and Andy opened the door. He stared at me, and suddenly looked overcome with embarrassment. "You'd better come in", he said. And as I entered the sitting room where Gail was seated, "It's Barrie. The dentist".

We talked. We drank coffee. They were new Christians. They had not been married long. Everything seemed more expensive than they had expected. Both worked, but bills were not getting paid because they did not have enough money.

I was a young dentist at the time, but their need was greater than mine. And they were my brother and sister in Christ. I told them to forget the bill. I suggested that they get advice on budgeting, and finance generally, and to explain their situation to any other creditors in case legal action was being considered.

I also advised them to have a chat with their church leaders about their position. We prayed together. Maybe I should have done more, but I was around thirty, and still had a lot to learn.

* * * * *

So often in life, I come back to Matthew 18:21-35 and the story of the wealthy king who was owed a large sum of money by a man who had no means with which to pay. The man asked for mercy, and the king forgave him the debt. Then the man went to someone who owed him a relatively small amount, and who was unable to pay him. Although his debtor asked for mercy, the creditor refused to forgive him, and had him thrown into prison. The king heard what had happened, retracted his forgiveness, and had his debtor thrown into prison where he was tormented.

There are several lessons here for Christians. The king is a picture of Jesus, and I am the man with the debt that cannot be paid. I have messed up and am beyond hope. Biblically, this is you too, by the way. The debt is huge, but Jesus pays the price on the cross. We cannot fully understand this, but are called to accept it. When we do - the debt is paid. The rightful sentence was eternal darkness, but I am spared. More than that, though not covered in this parable, I am adopted into the king's family. The point of the story is - what should my attitude be towards those who are indebted to me? There are those who owe me money. There are those who sin against me. What should my attitude be? How should I treat them?

I was very aware of this parable when I drove out to see Andy and Gail. Jesus had forgiven me so much; how mean I would be not to forgive a brother and sister a relatively small debt. Also, they could not pay.

Having said that, not every situation is so simple. Matt was not a believer, and so not a brother. He was out of work, but did not qualify for exemption from dental charges. Did he have savings? Or some other income? He had dental treatment from me, but did not pay. He was clearly a poor man, and I felt compassion. When he did not pay, I wrote and told him I had written off the debt. Then he came back with further dental problems. He needed more treatment because he was in pain. What would Jesus do? You have probably guessed - I carried out necessary treatment, and wrote off the debt. Later, Matt received government benefits that included free dental treatment, and so I treated him again and was paid by the State.

Do we have to write off all debts? Mrs. Adams came to my surgery and asked me to make her new dentures, privately. "Definitely private. I don't want rubbish". We agreed a fee, and I carried out the treatment. When she received the bill, she did not pay. After three months and three accounts, she still had not paid. Also, her daughter and son-in-law had now started courses of treatment with me. I suspected that I was just one more person the lady had treated that way. We asked the daughter and son-in-law to pay a deposit on their treatment. They refused. "Certainly not", they said indignantly. In this case I summonsed the lady to a court hearing, at which point the daughter and son-in-law cancelled all other appointments. The judge listened to her explanation, and then told her she was a villain. In response, she shouted rudely at the judge and accused him of bias. He threatened her with contempt of court. Why did I pursue her through the courts when the teaching of Matthew 18 suggests that I should forgive everybody?

In the chapter on *Wisdom*, I state that every scripture should be considered within the context of the whole Bible. We are called to have integrity and to live righteously, but also to exercise wisdom and prudence. We must each seek God's way, and search our hearts on these matters, and more fool us if we deceive ourselves or play games. I felt Mrs. Adams was preying on those supplying goods and services, and that was why I chose to prosecute. The judge awarded me my unpaid dental fees and a hefty amount of compensation. He was astounded when I waived the compensation, and he told Mrs. Adams that I was generous, though I am not sure she was very interested!

* * * * *

Jesus has paid our debt for us, so, how should we live? Once again, we're not talking about 'doing what the Bible says' or of ticking boxes. Heart attitude is at the centre of this issue. If Jesus has paid a debt of mine that I cannot pay, should I not have a similar attitude towards those who are indebted to me?

This book is about money, about finance, about pennies. But the actual context of Matthew 18 is much wider. It is about forgiveness in the broadest sense.

We are called to be generous, and one aspect of that is forgiveness. We live in a fallen world, and though we are divinely equipped to be 'more than conquerors', no-one is without sin. The world, the flesh and the devil each have their ways of seeking to bring us down, and people succumb. One result of this is that most people also have sins to forgive.

Someone once said, "Forgiveness is alright - until you have something to forgive". The theory sounds good, but when someone has betrayed you, or stolen from you, or offended you in a way that hurts deeply, the situation can be more than challenging. This can be especially acute in a marriage situation, and can lead to years, even a lifetime, of bitterness. Not only does the offended partner suffer the pain of betrayal, but where they feel unable or unwilling to forgive, there is the additional trauma of 'the torment' referred to in Matthew 18. Meditating on that parable, and the forgiveness extended to us by *the* King, and allowing the Holy Spirit to reveal the reality of this, can bring release and set a person totally free.

Forgiveness flows from grace, and comes at best, begrudgingly from a legalistic person. No Christian will claim to be without sin, except in Christ, but the legalist tends to think (and say), "Of course, we all sin, but I would never do *that*". Which leaves open the door to unforgiveness, and in turn, bitterness. Bitterness has been likened to drinking poison whilst hoping it will kill the other person. Bitterness does kill, but not 'the other person'.

We learn (if we're sensible) as we go through life. I have been the one asking forgiveness, and also the one extending it, even when it was not requested. I trust I have learnt grace in both these situations. Forgiveness is an expression of grace, love and kindness, and leads to bonding and unity. The converse is also true.

What is the answer? Jesus! If we appreciate the nature and extent of the debt we have been forgiven, we will not find it too difficult to forgive 'those who trespass against us'. It is difficult to imagine a generous person being resentful towards someone who has wronged them. We are called to extend generosity in every aspect of our lives.

* * * * *

The Bible says, *'Forgive us our debts as we also have forgiven our debtors'. Matthew 6:12.*

Chapter 16

It Just Ain't Fair!

John and Margaret are saints in every sense of the word. They are brilliant neighbours to those around them - and to those who live further afield. When my previous wife left me, a number of people said I must visit them for meals. Maybe half followed up with a date, and entertained me to supper or similar. But John and Margaret excelled, not only having me round for meals, but telephoning regularly to chat and generally be supportive. They have welcomed countless people to their home, and have even had a homeless person stay with them for some time. They serve tirelessly in their church. Their generosity is legendary. I could go on. But it just ain't fair!

Why do bad things happen to good people? John has had serious cardiac disease and surgery, has had cancer of the bowel, cancer of the skin, has dyslexia, and has already died once. By the grace of God, he was in hospital waiting for a routine appointment when he died of a cardiac arrest. Medics on hand brought him back. Margaret has had several accidents involving fractures and similar. Satnavs take them miles off route, and solar panels cause leaks, whilst one week later the company that fitted them goes bankrupt. They are not wealthy. I could go on, but my point is - it just ain't fair.

We live in a fallen world, which is a hostile environment. Satan and demonic powers seek to 'steal, kill and destroy' (John 10:10). I think people like John and Margaret are prime targets for Satan, as they share the gospel and carry out innumerable acts of kindness. I also know that they testify to the way their Heavenly Father has always provided for them, given them strength and joy, and enabled them to enjoy 'abundant life' (John 10:10) despite the seemingly relentless attacks of the evil one. There is a lot in this world that just ain't fair.

* * * * *

If you believe there are rules in this world whereby the good are rewarded with benefits, and the bad are rewarded with punishments, you can think again. The devil does not play by such rules, and is out to do all he can to prevent people entering the kingdom of God, disillusion those already in, and minimise its growth.

Jesus called Satan 'the prince of this world', (John 14:30) and he has a certain degree of authority. Those who have not trusted in Jesus are subject to Satan, whether they know it or not. He blinds people's minds to the truth (2 Corinthians 4:4). He causes suffering, such that people ask 'how can a God of love allow that?' He promotes and facilitates the dissemination of ungodly 'knowledge', such that people will mindlessly accept evolution, whilst ignoring questions such as 'where did life originate?', or 'what makes gravity work?' No-one has answered where life comes from, but God tells us in Genesis 1. In Colossians 1:17 we read that 'by him all things consist'. An encyclopaedia describes gravity as 'the glue that holds galaxies together', but no-one explains it. How does one species of animal or plant evolve into a totally different one? No-one explains, but people accept it, whilst ignoring creation. It ain't fair, but decent people's minds are blinded. It ain't fair, but decent people are going into a lost eternity. By human standards, it just ain't fair that Satan comes and steals, kills and destroys.

* * * * *

But Jesus does not play by the rules of this world either. The rules of the kingdom of God are very different from the rules of the world. The Lord brings salvation, success, prosperity, provision, joy and so many more good things, not to those who are good, decent people by the standards of this world - but to the *forgiven*.

Our God is holy and pure, and he created us to be holy and pure. Just one sin spoils holiness, and Adam's sin blighted the whole human race. We read in Romans 5:12 that it was by one man that sin entered the world. That sin of Adam's was passed on to all men. David speaks of being conceived 'in sin' (Psalm 51:5), and he was not referring to the marital state of his parents. He was born into humanity, which was impregnated throughout by sin.

And so however decent a person may be in this world, that person falls short of the holiness and purity that ensures fellowship with the God who is our great 'supply' in this life. Satan is the prince of this world, and the prince of all those born into it. He can do as he pleases with the people of this world (within the permit the Lord allows), and he can blind minds in so many ways.

But as I said above, Jesus does not play by the rules of this world either. We were without God and without hope, but we read that God so loved the world that he gave his only Son (John 3:16). Jesus was without sin, but he was punished for my sin. That just ain't fair. That is grace, and that is God. And from that sacrifice at Calvary flow the riches of heaven into our unworthy lives. Salvation, joy, health, strength, security, and the material wealth we enjoy - it is undeserved, it is by grace, and it just ain't fair.

Romans 5:15 tells us that although sin entered the world (and the human race) through one man, Adam, grace *abounds* through the sacrifice of Christ. At the start of this chapter I stated that John and Margaret did not deserve all the bad things that have happened to them, because they are such decent people. But there was a time when they did not know or trust Jesus. They were under the prince of this world (as we each have been until we came to Christ). However, when they came to put their trust in Jesus, their whole life changed. In fact, they testify to how good the Lord is to them, despite the attacks of the enemy. They would say that they are prospered by the Lord, having *every* need met – plus more. They will also speak of how they are in faith, that the Lord has even *more* good things for them. It just ain't fair, but that is what Jesus paid for at Calvary.

I consider myself to be even more undeserving, and I am sure there are those who must feel that it just ain't fair how good God has been to me. You know my story, if you have read part 1 of the book. I had no interest in the God who created me, and who so loved me that he gave his only Son for me. And yet he revealed himself to me, and blessed me beyond measure. He gave me the joys of wife and family, and of working with the Lord and the fulfilment that it brought, plus wealth a few years later. I did not deserve that. Then, after being blessed and favoured so lavishly, I let him down, let my family down and let the church down. And yet, when I turned back to him, he spoke to me clearly and gave me a commission to open a Christian bookshop and experience divine provision, a life lived with Jesus at my side, and a further experience of wealth in a way that was above the expectations of most people. *Fair?* Come on – that just ain't fair, but that *is* our God.

The Lord has made us many promises concerning our needs being met, of good health, and of success and prosperity. But these blessings are not deserved – they are a gift. And if we cannot earn them through being good, or keeping rules, then it follows that those who have really fallen, or have 'badly broken the rules', qualify equally. The riches of Christ are not for the good – they are for the *forgiven*. The world cannot understand this, though it is revealed so clearly in the Scriptures. *'All have sinned and fallen short of the glory of God', (Romans 3:23)*, and *'the wages of sin is death, but the free gift of God is eternal life'*, (Romans 6:23). And eternal life starts now, and includes all the blessings gained at Calvary. So whether you have failed, whatever people say about you, and even if your church has given up on you – make sure you are a forgiven person. Don't see yourself as disqualified, because the Lord does not bless good people – he blesses *forgiven* people. Make sure you are forgiven, and living a life faithful to your God. Turn to Jesus, and enjoy the life he extends to all.

* * * * *

Life in the kingdom of God is all about Jesus, and it is all through grace. Do I *deserve* my income? Do I *deserve* good health? Do I *deserve* the favour of my Heavenly Father to be upon me? No - but our Father delights to bless us in all these ways. And if we know these things to be true, what sort of people should we be? We should have an attitude of gratitude as we work with our Father to extend his kingdom here on earth, and honour the Son.

* * * * *

The Bible says, *'For you know the grace of our Lord Jesus Christ, that though he was rich, yet for your sake he became poor, so that you through his poverty might become rich'*. 2 Corinthians 8:9.

Chapter 17
True Love

I recently met a man who had worked hard for most of his life. I think he had played hard too. He had certainly built up quite a fortune. But now in his latter years, some business partners had cheated him, and he has nothing. He is a sad man.

* * * * *

Citizen Kane regularly appears towards the top of lists of the best films ever made. It is a fascinating story, based on a true life character, who worked in the newspaper industry, and reached the very top with an amazing fortune. The end of the film is memorable, as he sadly reminisces about *Rosebud*. Watch the film! Despite his wealth, he ends up a desperately depressed man.

* * * * *

Matthew 6:24 is such a meaningful verse. We cannot serve two masters - and yet there are two who might be seen as competing for our affection. The question is - who or what do we love the most, Jesus or money?

"Jesus, of course", we say, almost reflexly. But do we? How can we really know? There are, in fact, two tests that will give us a much more objective appraisal on this issue. Perhaps "Jesus, of course", is just talking the talk. It is a subjective assessment based on... what exactly? Our thoughts or assumptions, or what we have always said? It might simply be what we want others to hear, and think. But we can be more objective.

I have written in chapter 1 that there are two things that we can spend however we like - but we can spend them once only. When they are gone, they are gone. Forever. It is important that we understand this, and so I will repeat it! We can spend time in any way that we like. The choice is ours. But we can only spend it once. You have ten minutes, or an hour, or... but once spent, it is gone forever. In fact, we have a lifetime - how will we spend it? Just now, you have chosen to read this book. How will you spend your other time? We tend to spend time doing what we *want* to do. There is much less of a sense of *duty* to do things now we are in the twenty-first century, whereas in the mid-twentieth century, people in general were more principled. So, do what you like - and do what you choose to do.

We spend time with people that we love and with things that we love. I spend a lot of time with my wife Wendy, because that is something I really enjoy. I also like to please her, and I know that she likes us spending time together. But I also know people who are car enthusiasts, often classic cars of a particular marque, and they spend hours and hours with their car and others. Being a fan of a football team hardly needs a mention. But if I say I love Jesus, am I being consistent and spending time with him?

Money is really the subject of this book, and for many people, it is a god. The possession of money seems to offer so much. But having money itself is not condemned as sinful in the Bible. The Lord gave Abraham great wealth, and likewise some Christians in the New Testament. *Love* of money, however, is clearly identified not only as wrong, but the root of so many other evils as well (1 Timothy 6:10). Theft, dishonesty, cheating, lying, murder and many other actions which are evil in themselves, so often flow from the love of money. Loving the Lord is the first commandment, but for many, money is too strong a competitor.

How do I spend my money? Am I number one? What are my priorities when it comes to using it? Does Jesus have a big say in what goes where? Much of this is covered in another chapter, but the choice between God and 'mammon' is important. And telling.

In Luke 16:9, we read the words 'mammon of unrighteousness' and in Luke 16:11, 'unrighteous mammon'. Mammon is best translated wealth, and money is the god that seems to promise to open the door to material wealth. Money and wealth are not wrong in themselves (I have already mentioned that the Lord gave tremendous wealth to Abraham, David, Solomon and many people in the New Testament, as well as to people today), but when they become a god, or are obtained dishonestly, they are 'unrighteous'. And people chase after wealth, and having gained it (for some do), they remain unfulfilled, and chase after more. Ecclesiastes 5:10 reads, 'Whoever loves money never has enough'. For some, it is an addiction that destroys them. Others are convicted of dishonesty in their passion for it, and are publicly disgraced. One can read such accounts in the newspapers almost daily.

Let us consider why people chase after money, and make it their god. There are two things that money would appear to offer – fulfilment and security.

Fulfilment.

Unsaved man is unfulfilled. We were created for a relationship with our Heavenly Father, and once cut off from that, man is unfulfilled. He is restless, feeling somehow incomplete. And so he starts seeking, dreaming, imagining what will bring satisfaction into his, or her, life.

For some it is a better home – larger, or in a better location, or more attractive, or whatever. Others believe that if they take a certain holiday (often called 'the holiday of a lifetime'), they will then feel they have arrived. Or maybe a new gadget, the latest mobile phone, seeing their football team promoted (and then?), the car they have always dreamed of – the list is endless. The access to the goal is usually money, but the realization of it disappoints in that one is still unfulfilled.

Mammon is things that the world offers. Money is usually involved, and can become the big focus in life. But although the world promises so much, it never delivers. Only a relationship with the Father through the Son brings real fulfilment. And once one enters into that, fulfilment is attained, and so much more is added. I found in my thirties that the trappings of material wealth did not bring satisfaction, but instead brought disaster. My experience might have been extreme, but in essence that is shared by all who seek fulfilment from money and things. The converse is also true, in that having lost most of my wealth, I found fulfilment in my relationship with my Heavenly Father, and that really satisfied. Following that, there was a restoration of wealth. Not that I am a millionaire or enjoy the lifestyle of a millionaire, though I do not believe that a millionaire could enjoy life more than I do.

In Luke 15, we have the story generally referred to as 'The Prodigal Son'. The younger of two sons takes his inheritance prematurely, and goes away into the world where he uses it to seek pleasure. He can afford lots of 'things', and he is in a position to indulge in promiscuous sexual activity. Such a lifestyle is generally promoted through the media as being wildly exciting, and to be desired. But the reality of the situation is very different. In the parable of the prodigal son, he ended up as a casual labourer, eating the food for which he was paid to feed pigs. He was distraught and about as unfulfilled as one can get. Likewise for so many people who chase after money and then use it for a life of obtaining things and living in a promiscuous manner. The result is dissatisfaction and disillusionment, often accompanied by depression. The use of drugs is widespread, and simply compounds the problem. In similar fashion to the prodigal son, life is worse than disappointing.

But the story of the prodigal son does not end in the pigsty. He comes to his senses, and returns to his father. He is welcomed. There is a party. He is restored, with quality clothes, a gold ring, and family status again. At last, he finds fulfilment. The message of Jesus' teaching here is quite clear, in that we can go as far from our Heavenly Father as is possible, but will never find fulfilment in doing so. However, returning to Him brings satisfaction in a way that nothing else can. Having been a member of the Full Gospel Businessmen's Fellowship for many years, I have heard innumerable real life stories of men who have totally messed up. Some were from wealthy backgrounds, and some from circumstances of extreme poverty. Most are just normal everyday people like you and me. They tell of how they looked for satisfaction in the various ways that the world offers, chasing after mammon and indulging in a multitude of activities in order to try to find fulfilment. Some became extremely wealthy, and obtained very senior positions in industry, the military or the world of sport. Others became involved in crime, often related to drugs, and spent many years in prison. They all had certain things in common - none found satisfaction in this life, through status, wealth, drugs, sex, or anything else. Each heard the gospel message, and responded. In doing so, they came into a relationship with God as their father, and never looked back again. Well, one or two did glance back, and faltered. But having learnt from that, they then moved strongly back into the relationship which delivered what nothing else on earth is capable of – fulfilment. I have listened to so many such testimonies, and have entertained so many such people in our home, and their story is in essence very much like my own. Chase after wealth, and you will end up a disappointed person.

Seek God – indeed, chase after him – and you will know a joy that gives strength during life's darkest hours, and which will bring satisfaction in this life, way beyond anything that you ever thought possible.

Security.

The other prize that is held out by the world is that of security. If we go back to the beginning again, man was created for a relationship with God as his Heavenly Father. When man sinned, he became frightened. When he heard the Lord walking in the Garden, he hid. This speaks to us of fear and of insecurity, and is common to all people. We might learn to wear a brave face, and we might even kid ourselves, but fear of death is referred to in the Bible as being common to all (Hebrews 2:15). There is also widespread fear of being inadequate, and of being in some way inferior to others, and this is quite common amongst those who have significant wealth.

What is the world's answer to insecurity? Wealth, property, financial policies, and so on. And how do you get them? Money! But once again, the world just does not deliver. However much money you have, you will always want more. I have found that to be true, and it is common to all. Again I remind you of Ecclesiastes 5:10, which tells us, 'Whoever loves money never has enough; whoever loves wealth is never satisfied with their income'. The security that wealth brings can be short-lived. Men who have been seen as giants of British industry and commerce have suddenly vanished from the scene. The disillusionment that comes when financial security is realised to be far from secure, has led a number of people to suicide.

True love can be expressed towards money and wealth in general – but it will not be returned. Jesus said that he alone has come to bring real life with all the satisfaction people long for. Satan comes to 'steal, kill and destroy' people's lives, and does so by deceiving them with the lure of mammon. Thank God for Jesus.

Fulfilment and Security Guaranteed.

But despite the deception and false hope of both fulfilment and security dangled before a disappointed and dissatisfied world, there is an answer, with a capital 'J'.

Satan has always mimicked the one true God, and has masqueraded as such. He deceives people into thinking that he has the answer, and he draws them after himself – to destruction. You will probably have heard of the time when Moses and Aaron went to Pharaoh in Egypt, and presented him with the word of God, "Let my people go". Pharaoh would not entertain this, and a succession of signs and wonders, a number of them plagues and similar, then took place. One of the early signs was that Aaron threw his rod onto the ground. It changed into a serpent. This was a demonstration of the power of God. The magicians of Egypt then threw their rods onto the ground, and they too became serpents. From whence did they get the power to do this? Satan mimics the true God, and he is not without power. However, Aaron's serpent then consumed those of the magicians (Exodus 7:8-13). The power of God will always prevail against the enemy.

Likewise with fulfilment and security. The world, the flesh and the devil seem to offer so much, but it is deception. Only the true God can offer real fulfilment, and only He can offer true security. The Bible bears witness to this throughout, and men and women of God testify to this in their own personal experience.

I have written my own story, largely from the perspective of finance, in the first part of this book. Have you noticed the disaster of seeking fulfilment from wealth, and the realisation of satisfaction in life through my relationship with my Heavenly Father? Have you also noticed the security I sense and am convinced of through that relationship. That is our God. That is what Jesus has brought.

And with Jesus, there is always more! There is fulfilment and security, but there is also the assurance of every need being met. So many Bible verses state this as a promise, and two (one from the Old Testament and one from the New) are Psalm 23:1 and Philippians 4:19.

But there is always more, and 3 John 2, along with many other verses, speak of the Lord's will to prosper us – to meet every need, and also to see that there is more.

* * * * *

I want to bring two Bible verses to your attention as I draw this chapter to a conclusion.

Proverbs 11:28, (NLT). 'Trust in your money and down you go'. I love the way some modern translations bring a sharper edge to some of the more familiar older translations. But this verse, as expressed above, is so true. If you trust in your money, you will go down. There is a war on, and you can trust in God or you can trust in money and wealth. If you do not place your trust in God, 'down you go'. Down you go in this world, certainly in your satisfaction level, and maybe in other ways too. And down you go in the world to come. Heaven and hell are spoken of by Jesus as real places, and Christians are remiss if they fail to mention this vital truth.

So, remember – *Trust in your money, and down you go!*

The second verse is found in Luke 16:11. 'And if you are untrustworthy about worldly wealth, who will trust you with the true riches of heaven?' We all have to handle worldly wealth. We use money every day, and we have all sorts of worldly wealth that has been entrusted to us. We have homes, means of transport, food, and so on. This verse makes it clear that we have been entrusted with these things, and the Lord looks for faithfulness. With our money, are we putting Jesus first? Are we seeking his will in how we give, spend and save? With our homes and other possessions, are we mean or generous? Is your front door open, and are there invitations to your table? It is not the food, but the hospitality.

I know many Christians who would love to be in a place of leadership and of 'ministry'. I also know many who do occupy such places. There are manmade systems of 'church' where people who aspire to such position and function can earn their way. But in Luke 16:11, the Lord makes it quite clear that if anyone desires to be entrusted with real ministry from heaven, then they must first be found faithful in the areas of money and wealth.

If you are faithful with your money, and with the material possessions with which the Lord has entrusted you, then he will further entrust you with the true riches of heaven. It comes back to the big contest that Jesus alluded to in Matthew 6:24 – we cannot serve two masters. We will ultimately serve one. We may pay lip service to the other, but we will serve one. And if we want to enjoy the riches of heaven in this life and the next, we will do well to remember Luke 16:11.

If you are untrustworthy about worldly wealth, who will trust you with the true riches of heaven?

* * * * *

What an amazing Heavenly Father we have, and what a Friend we have in Jesus. True love – to whom, or to what, do you express true love? God or mammon?

True love – *'For God so loved the world, that he gave his one and only Son, that whoever believes in him shall not perish but have eternal life'*. If God so loved us, and if Jesus hung and suffered there on the cross for us, what should be our response? There can only be one for those who love him.

* * * * *

The Bible says, *'No man can serve **two masters**: for either he will hate the one, and love the other; or else he will hold to the one, and despise the other. Ye cannot serve **God and mammon**'. Matthew 6:24*

Chapter 18

When It All Goes Wrong!

I have been there – twice. I know something about life when it all goes wrong. It happens, and sometimes quite unexpectedly, which intensifies the pain.

* * * * *

Gordon walked to the microphone, and gazed across the restaurant at those of us who had just enjoyed a superb dinner. He gave an engaging smile and said, "I haven't done this before, but I want to tell you all how Jesus has changed my life".

That was back in 1990. Gordon had given his life to Jesus in 1972 and everything had changed. He was a businessman, and an enterprising, hard-working one too, supplying market gardens with their various requirements. He prospered. What could go wrong for Gordon? The answer is – he was defrauded, and years of industrious, creative labour and investment, and even pensions, were stripped from him. Try and imagine what that is like. How would you react? Let me tell you how Gordon handled it.

He and his wife Jackie were determined to put Jesus first in their lives. Soon after they came to know him, he had given them a clear promise that he would always be their provider. He had been so during the good times, and they knew they could depend on him during the bad times. They also felt that they should not 'count money', and have not done so for forty years. (That was God's way for Gordon and Jackie. It is not for me, and probably not for you, the reader).

Today Gordon deals in antiques, but spends much time, as ever, about the Lord's work, not to mention serving the community through local government. He is also a great strength and encourager to me personally in my work with the Full Gospel Businessmen.

* * * * *

I grew up in a stable loving home. My parents were not wealthy, and sometimes life was very difficult for them financially. But I enjoyed my childhood, and assumed that life would generally be rather like my parents' had been. Other people experienced financial disasters, (how embarrassing), but things like that did not happen in our family. There were people who got divorced (disgrace, shame and scandal in those days), but such things never happened to us. I would no doubt marry and have a family – I assumed a boy and a girl, like my parents – and then grow old gracefully, enjoying the grandchildren, who would live locally.

Training to be a dentist took much of the family by surprise. I thought it was just a 'job' I wanted to do, and only later realised it was a 'profession' with, in the eyes of some, status. My father was a bank clerk, and his father worked on the railway. I was going to be a dentist. Just jobs.

The big surprise for me was discovering that I had a Heavenly Father who loved me. I had thought it was wishful thinking on the part of the gullible, and when I realised the truth, and committed myself to him, life became a tremendous adventure.

What wonderful promises we find in the Bible, not least in the general area of success, and also in the specific sphere of money. Every need shall be met, I read in Psalm 23:1 and

Philippians 4:19 and so many other places in the Bible. Psalms and Proverbs abounded with promises of success and prosperity, and there were demonstrations of the realization of it in the lives of Abraham, Isaac, Jacob, Esau, Joseph, David, Solomon, Joseph of Arimathea, Philemon and others. I did not expect to be wealthy myself, but with so many promises, there was not too much that could really go wrong.

I have mentioned several times that every scripture needs to be taken within the context of the rest of the Bible. There is also a big picture in the Bible, going back before creation and continuing into future eternity, and part of that picture is sin, the Fall, sickness, disease, disobedience, poverty, dishonesty, infidelity and of a perfect creation becoming a hostile environment.

Sickness happens. Unemployment happens. Infidelity happens. Dishonesty happens. There is so often a financial consequence to these aspects of our fallen world, whether one is the sinner, or the sinned-against. And we rarely see them coming, and get taken by surprise.

Life comes in seasons. The promise of abundant life is there for us, but that does not mean that the enemy will not attack, seeking to steal, to kill and to destroy (John 10:10). Victory is assured, but wounds can be sustained in the battle. Job started well and the Lord prospered him. Later in his life, we read again that Job was prospering, having twice as much as he did in his earlier days. But it is the in-between years that made Job famous. He lost his family and material possessions, along with his health. However, Job remained faithful to the Lord, who brought him through, eventually, into something even better than before.

We too can have a 'Job experience'. But if you are going to have a Job experience, remain faithful to the Lord as Job did, and have a complete Job experience, coming through into something even better than you had before.

So, when it all goes wrong, how do we handle life? I have found certain Biblical principles which need to be followed, and which, by the grace of God, *can* be followed. I have known too many people give up because the way ahead seemed difficult. Don't give up. I have seen too many people go into depression because they felt the enemy could not be overcome. Refuse to think that way – our God is greater. And I have seen too many people becoming, and remaining, bitter and resentful at others, because they have been sinned against. Don't even think about it – the Lord has forgiven you far more than you will ever have to forgive anyone else. That is the teaching of Matthew 18:21-35.

As a younger man, I made mistakes and 'it all went wrong'. I felt that everything was taken from me. I did not go bankrupt, but I bounced along on the fine line between credit and debit on my bank account. I learnt from my mistakes, and the mistakes of others, and even though I did not prosper to the extent of some people I know, I enjoyed good fellowship with Jesus and the people of God – and life was good.

Later, as an older man, someone else made mistakes and 'it all went wrong'. I was just getting on my feet again financially when – I was plundered. What a wonderful Heavenly Father we have! I will never understand how he brought me through, and restored and re-established me so quickly and to the extent that he has. Suffice to say that, after some months of extreme challenge, life has been good for the last sixteen years or so.

God is good, but there are principles to hold to. Let me briefly share a few of them with you.

Put Jesus first.

'Seek first the kingdom of God and all these things will be added to you', (Matthew 6:33). Jesus gives us instruction and a promise. The instruction is practical; in other words, he is telling us something we should *do*. You will recall perhaps that I have said that walking the walk is much more important than talking the talk. Put Jesus first, with both your time and your money.

Whatever else you do each day, spend time with Jesus. There is always time for what we *want* to do. Put time aside, and get away from possible distractions. Turn off your mobile phone, and stay away from your computer, telephone, television or whatever constitutes a possible distraction for you. Read a short passage, perhaps a psalm, and pause – what is the Lord saying to you? Is there a lesson to learn, or a promise to embrace? Believe me, it will be relevant to your situation because that is our God. He is our Father and he loves us. Then pray, responding to what he has just said to you. This time with the Lord is your lifeline. This is the time when he will speak joy, hope and strength into you, body, soul and spirit, to keep you going, and to bring you through.

Make Jesus Lord of your money! Thank him for what you have, and push some of it his way. Don't just laugh and say, "I haven't got any!" Everybody has something, and he only expects us to give proportionately (1 Corinthians 16:2). Do not give to the Lord in order to receive something greater back; just give to him in gratitude for what he has given you, and to acknowledge that he is Lord of your money. You are going to come through this time, and you are going to have a lot more in the future.

Move on.

Remember Lot's wife (Luke 17:32). She looked back – and died. There is a right way of looking back, and a wrong way of looking back. The correct, healthy way is to look back and thank God for all he has done, to see how far you have come, and of the lessons learned. But most people look back in an unhealthy manner. There can be a tendency to blame others, which leads to bitterness and resentment. That will at best leave you stuck where you are, and will more than likely drag you back. Consider how much the Lord has forgiven you, and forgive others. Again, remember the parable of the forgiven debtor of Matthew 18:21-35. If you can really take on board the meaning and truth of this teaching, it will set you wonderfully free. The first time it really went wrong for me, I felt resentful at the part others had played, even though I was a prime respondent. But I try and learn as I go through life, and so, the second time it went wrong for me, I freely forgave. It took a few months to have complete peace, but there was, and is, no resentment. When I received news that things had gone very badly wrong for my former wife, I sat down and wept my heart out. I felt no romantic attraction towards her any more, but I do not like to hear of people suffering.

Accepting responsibility for your part in things going wrong, is complementary to not blaming others. Or maybe you are perfect? I used to know a man who would relate certain business disasters that had befallen him. There seemed to have been a succession of such failures over many decades, and guess what? It was always 'them others'! It is not that he had exercised bad judgment, nor that he had moved ahead without fully appraising the situation, nor… He was a serial victim, and I was always hearing about the injustices of many years previously. But, it held him back. You will probably have noticed that in my own story, I accept that I was wrong in the breakdown of my first marriage. Nor do I believe that I was perfect in the following marriage. I acknowledge my shortcomings and learn from them, get right with God, and knowing that he has forgiven me, I forgive myself and move on. Accept ownership of wrong decisions and actions – learn from them and forgive yourself. Your Heavenly Father has. Jesus paid the price for them at Calvary. So forgive yourself, and move on.

Go to church!

I do not think anyone who knows me would call me legalistic, but if I can press you into going to a decent church during good *and* bad times, you can call me what you like. Do not drop out – it could be the end of you.

When I and my first wife separated, I lived for a few weeks in rented accommodation in a small village. I felt a total failure, and not a little depressed. But I walked along to the chapel about half a mile away, and though it was rather stuffy and formal, I sang to my God and sought to meet him there. I did not make any lifelong buddies amongst the very elderly congregation, but it was good to identify with the people of God, and worship.

The enemy comes to steal, to kill and destroy, and if he can separate you from the people of God, he will pick you off in his own good time. Remember how the Amalekites would pick off the weak and the stragglers who had separated themselves from the main body of the people of Israel as they crossed the Sinai desert in Deuteronomy 25:17-19. I have seen too many people drop out of church because they 'have not felt like it' whilst going through a bad time. Maybe they never understood commitment in the first place, or maybe they were never really saved. Years later one meets them again, unexpectedly in the street or in a shop, and they look a little embarrassed, and sometimes say, "I still believe in God". Well, so does Satan, and he is not going to pull through. But you are, if you really are a child of God. So do not drop out. Your future prosperity will flow from the inside out, and it is of paramount importance that your soul prospers, as in 3 John 2.

Whilst on the subject of dropping out of church, I have noticed that those who do so tell themselves that it is just for a while. But as the weeks, and then months slip by, they adopt a routine for their Sunday mornings – visiting family, going to car boot sales, watching football, and so on. A year or two later, it is no longer practical for them to join with church on Sundays because they are doing other things. The enemy steals, kills and destroys. Do not let him do that to you. Stay with the people of God, because that is what your Heavenly Father desires (Hebrews 10:25). It is a safe place.

Praise him!

I think I have always praised God, since I first came to know him at the age of twenty-one. But there was a time when, for a few months, I suffered from clinical depression. I was a young married man, and I felt very down. But praise lifted me. Did I feel like praising him? No. Was it easy to praise him? No. In fact often, I would not even think of praising the Lord. I overcame this by handwriting notes for myself, when the depression lifted for a while, and I could think rationally. The notes would say 'Praise the Lord – sing!' I would find the notes when I was 'down', sing around the house, and emerge from my depression. Praise brings deliverance.

Remember Jehoshaphat. In 2 Chronicles 20:22 we have a curious incident in the history of Judah. Three strong, hostile nations, Ammon, Moab and Edom combined their armies to fight against Judah. The king of Judah, Jehoshaphat, adopted an unusual strategy, in sending out ahead of the army, not spearmen nor chariots nor soldiers of any description – but singers to praise the Lord. And when they praised the Lord, He brought confusion to their enemies, who were routed. Our God does not change – praise the Lord and send the enemy packing. You are going to come through, but you need to move in victory. Praise him!

I have a good friend called Mike, who himself had a friend called Merlin. Mike was not going through the best of times, but his friend had recently written a book called *Prison to Praise*, and Mike read it. Merlin had written of the power of praise (the title of another of his books) in releasing God's people from an inner prison and setting them free. Mike decided that he was going to do just that. He may not have felt like it, but he was determined to praise the Lord whatever his circumstances. His train arrived at their home station at the end of a day's work in the city. Tired, he trudged from the station, to find his daughter running along the road towards him. "Daddy, Daddy", she cried. "Our house has been struck by lightning". Without hesitation, Mike threw his arms in the air and shouted, "Praise the Lord!" (Apparently there was a hole in the roof the size of a double-decker bus!)

You are going to come through, but you need to move in victory. Praise him! His will is for you to succeed and prosper on all fronts. Remember Jehoshaphat. Remember Mike. Praise the Lord!

Exercise prudence and wisdom

Some years ago I had a young friend who went through a difficult time both financially and emotionally. He came to see me for a general time of catching up on each other's news and was clearly excited. "I've found a great scheme for making money", he said. "Join me in it. Twenty or thirty grand, and it will double, at least, in just a few months". I told him that if a scheme looks too good to be true, then it almost certainly is too good to be true. And if I had twenty or thirty thousand pounds to invest, it would not go into something like that. Not many months later, I heard that he had gone bankrupt, which was so sad.

The book of Proverbs has a lot to say about prudence and wisdom. Prudence means common sense. Wisdom is perhaps somewhat deeper, and suggests insight and perception. Most people have common sense if they stop and think, but a smaller number of people possess wisdom.

'I wisdom, dwell with prudence', reads Proverbs 8:12. Wisdom is personified in this chapter, and is a picture of Christ. We are 'in Christ' and Christ is 'in us'. If you need common sense and wisdom, you have it, if you are a believer. So use it!

But when it all goes wrong, there is an understandable temptation to try and get out of the situation quickly. Pause. Think. Use common sense and wisdom. If you have a bad track record when it comes to such matters, discuss your situation with an older and wiser person who can be trusted. And if a scheme looks too good to be true, do not go near it.

There have been times when I have had some degree of pastoral responsibility, and there have also been times when patients have opened their heart to me because everything has been going wrong for them. Such times often involved divorce or bereavement. There are usually financial considerations. In such situations I would suggest that, due to the emotional turmoil experienced, it was not advisable to do any of the following three things within one year, absolute minimum: change your work, move your home, or get married. Surely that is common sense, and yet I have seen so many people in those situations get married very quickly – and regret it. Quite often, a further divorce, with further trauma, follows. A downward spiral involving both bad health and financial embarrassment can result.

If it all goes wrong, hang in. Find one or two wise people, experienced in life and who truly love God, and share your situation with them. And remember, you will come through.

In debt, and getting worse?

Whatever your situation in life, your relationship with Jesus is your lifeline. This is true however good things are (a dangerous time - see next chapter), and especially during potentially desperate times.

Sometimes people, including Christians, find themselves becoming engulfed in ever-increasing debt. There are a variety of causes, and the interest payable on a debt can add significantly to the amount owed, which can then cause it to increase exponentially. It can escalate. Suddenly, the situation seems hopeless. But no situation is hopeless. Nothing is impossible with our God (Matthew 19:26). Is anything too hard for the Lord? (Genesis 18:14). Don't limit the Holy One of Israel (Psalm 78:41). But remember - your relationship with Jesus and your Heavenly Father is your lifeline. And apply the principles I have covered in this chapter.

However, if this is your situation, I would strongly advise availing yourself of free Christian professional advice. I have seen many people in the UK set free from debt, and then prospering, through the work of Christians Against Poverty (CAP). They are professional, and therefore competent. They are Christian, and so they are caring, and bring the love of God into their work. They are non-judgmental, and therefore very user-friendly. And they are free. CAP have helped friends of mine get out of debt and stay out of debt. I have seen unbelievers turn to Christ, though CAP is not evangelistic. I commend them to you if you need help. They can be contacted by phone, and found through the Internet.

Remember the promises.

Never forget the promises. The Bible is full of promises from our loving Heavenly Father, and he is as good as his word. I do not want to waste my life believing things that are not true, but neither do I want to miss out by not believing the things that are true.

There are books of Bible promises, or they can easily be found on the Internet. I am not strongly in favour of 'claiming them', but have a familiarity with them, and simply believe them. Life has seasons and some of those seasons are not full of success and prosperity. Remember Job. But life in general is good, because God is my Father, and he promises me success and prosperity. If this is not so, then the Bible is not true. Or my theology is suspect. But the Bible *is* God's word, and is true, as are *all* the promises (2 Corinthians 1:20)

And so in closing this chapter, I have a few simple suggestions for you.

Read Psalm 1, where there is a promise of success and prosperity for those who live a life of commitment to the Lord.
Read Psalm 23 where there are true and comforting words about your great Shepherd.
Read Psalm 121 and remember your help comes from the Lord.
Read Philippians 4:19, and remember that this is speaking of what the Lord promises *you*.
Read 3 John 2, and remember that our God does not change.

Meditate on the promises.
Remember that the promises have not been withdrawn.
Remember that our God does not change (Malachi 3:6), and that Jesus is the same yesterday, today and forever (Hebrews 13:8).
Praise God for the promises.
Remind God of the promises.

And remember that if you walk with the Lord, he will bring you through into something better. Remember Job. Remember me. Praise him!

* * * * *

The Bible says, *'I will restore to you the years that the swarming locust has eaten, the crawling locust, the consuming locust, and the chewing locust'*, Joel 2:25

Chapter 19

When It All Goes Right!

I have been there - twice. It's a good place to be, compared with 'when it all goes wrong'. It's a blessed place to be, but - it's also a dangerous place. Looking back over more than fifty years of Christian life, I feel that I have handled the years of austerity better than I have the years of relative wealth. The more you have, the greater the temptations.

A friend of mine has been mightily blessed by God, and over a period of time, I would seriously guess, has accumulated hundreds of millions of pounds to his name. "Why him and not me?" I asked the Lord, with my tongue in my cheek. The answer which I felt I heard from heaven was, "Because I can trust him". Observing his lifestyle, I see godly living, with generosity to individuals, projects and communities. I suspect that what I have observed is just the tip of the iceberg. Also, I believe his Heavenly Father is pleased to see him enjoying what he has given him. I would with my kids.

But when riches come, there are strong temptations and dangers.

* * * * *

In Proverbs 30:7-9, we read, "Two things I ask of you, LORD; do not refuse me before I die: keep falsehood and lies far from me; give me neither poverty nor riches, but give me only my daily bread. Otherwise, I may have too much and disown you and say, 'Who is the LORD?' Or I may become poor and steal, and so dishonor the name of my God".

I am not sure that is a prayer for everyone, but certainly Agur son of Jakeh wanted to be spared the temptations associated with both poverty and wealth, though temptation is common to all, regardless of whether one is poor or wealthy, or indeed, somewhere between those two extremes.

During a time of relative poverty (and poverty might well have a different definition according to country and time), there are temptations to acquire money through dishonest means. In the UK, one reads in the newspapers of people taking government benefits when they are not entitled to them. Some of these people are far from poor, and that is a temptation that I personally have not experienced. Indeed, it is difficult for many in middle-class England to appreciate what it is to be poor. Our Full Gospel Businessmen's Fellowship in Norwich is involved with feeding the homeless, and to mix with such people can be quite a revelation. During my 'lean years', especially whilst at university, the temptation to covet was almost irresistible, especially before I came to know Jesus. For most of my student days, I walked and had no spare cash, and yet some of my peers drove expensive sports cars.

The temptation Agur associated with wealth, was to disown God. For those whose lives have been radically changed by an encounter with Jesus, this may seem an unlikely temptation to face, and yet it is very subtle. One can continue with the routine of reading the Bible, praying and attending church, with involvement in Christian activity, and yet it might be just that – *routine*. We each need to maintain a living relationship with the Lord, and even then there will be temptation for the wealthy to trust, to a greater or lesser extent, in themselves. And that, I believe, was the cause of my troubles which resulted in me losing so much whilst still a relatively young man.

Reading through the history of Israel, and especially Judah, we find that it is unusual for the people to be completely devoted to the Lord, or completely devoted to heathen gods. There was so often a mixture, where Asherah poles would exist alongside altars to the Lord. We see this in some countries today, where missionaries have taken the gospel, but compromised with local heathen religions, leaving the people with an amalgamation of the two. This can happen to us, and the temptation to trust in the Lord partially, and also to trust in money, is obvious.

I found increased wealth difficult to handle in my younger days. I was not used to it, and although I was very involved in church and Christian work, I was also involved in the world of dentistry, and spending time with people who were fairly wealthy and who usually had no Christian commitment. Maybe something of their values rubbed off onto me, which I should have guarded against. Most of us need close Christian fellowship, and accountability to others in the church. Having money gives a degree of independence, in that one can travel more and further, and as a result, spend less time in close fellowship with church and those to whom one is accountable.

The words of Solomon in Ecclesiastes 5:10 are so true. 'Whoever loves money will never have enough money. Whoever loves luxury will not be content with abundance'. The world, the flesh and the devil seem to offer so much – but they never deliver, and they never satisfy. If making a fortune is your goal in life, you will never be free from the slavery that entails. If you simply want to 'have enough', you will probably find that you never reach that place of having enough. The more you have, the more you want. So warns Solomon in Ecclesiastes, and that is most certainly a temptation to be aware of, and to resist.

Pride is a common temptation of the wealthy. When everything is going right for us, we can be proud of ourselves. That is sin. The wealthy can easily come to despise the poor, and in similar fashion, the poor can despise the wealthy. The poor are 'idiots and lazy' and the wealthy are 'idiots, privileged and undeserving'. These attitudes tend to be expressed to quite a degree through party politics. Such an attitude is completely unacceptable in the life of a Christian. Every person on this earth is created in the image of God, and although that image is marred by sin to a greater or lesser extent, we should regard others with a basic dignity.

I think the psalmist summarises the great temptation that comes with wealth. 'Though your riches increase, do not set your heart on them', Psalm 62:10. That is the big danger, and we have all seen it in others so many times. So let's have a look at how we can guard against it.

I have written earlier that there are certain principles that we need to apply to our lives with regard to money. They are all important in all circumstances, but some are more applicable when everything is going right.

Acknowledge the source.

All good gifts come from God (James 1:17), and I believe that includes our wealth. There is temptation to have a 'haven't I done well' attitude, and there will be those who tell us that we 'deserve' what we have. But when it is all going right, there are usually others who have done as much as we have, and for whom it is not going right. When everything is going right, we are being *blessed*. It is by *grace*. Let us confess that it is the blessing of God, and we are a beneficiary of his goodness.

Put Jesus first.

When everything is going right, there can be temptation to put other things ahead of Jesus. Work can take priority over everything else - leisure, family, spouse and Jesus. To be working all hours is a probable indication that the scripture, 'whoever loves money will never have enough money' (Ecclesiastes 5:10) needs to be considered. If Jesus is Lord, do not let work squeeze him out. If you love your wife/husband, don't let your work squeeze them out. Or your children.

I really enjoyed my work as a dentist, meeting a wide variety of people, examining teeth to see what was wrong, explaining disease processes and treatments to patients, and answering questions. Also, treating the teeth. Painlessly, of course! There was enough demand for me to have worked all hours, but I did not. I was always home in time for supper, and my wife and I would spend time reading to our children, before having a praise song, a short Bible story, and a time when we each prayed briefly.

I added more surgeries to the practice and took on other dentists to help with the work. I did not have to work all hours. When my income started to soar, I reduced my hours and worked with the church a day or more a week. Not everything worked out, but putting Jesus first is a *practical* matter, and not just something we say. When everything is going right, work can take over.

Or other things can take over. With increased wealth one can get away more. Weekends, short breaks, a holiday home... Once again, priorities can be the issue. Where does Jesus come? Church is an integral part of the Christian life, and is an important consideration.

Put Jesus first with both your time and your money. I will not repeat what I have written earlier, but the temptation to prioritise other things when it comes to the allocation of time and money, is very real when everything is going well financially.

Ask yourself, 'Why?'

If we rightly acknowledge that the Lord is the source of all the good things that we have, it will be helpful to pause and ask ourselves why he has given us wealth. We have looked at this in chapter 10, but it is worth personalising the reasons the Lord has given *me* (you, in fact), wealth.

He has given me wealth to help extend his kingdom. How exactly? Where do I channel my financial giving to achieve this? Where in this country? In particular areas of the church of which I am a part? Where abroad? Of what has the Lord made me aware recently, or longer ago? What areas and aspects of the kingdom of God really concern me?

He has given us wealth in order that we might bless others. Why has he given you wealth now, you can ask yourself? And ask him. Are there people in your family who need help? In your church? Other Christians you have been made aware of? Other people? Are there charities that carry out work that pulsates with your own spiritual heartbeat? Asking yourself such questions, and praying around them, can be useful. Bequeathing to fellowships, churches, missions, etc. should also be considered when making a will. (And make sure you do make a will, for the sake of those you love). Finally, on this subject, don't forget to be spontaneous.

When I give money to my children and grandchildren, I would like to think they act along similar lines to those I have outlined. But I also want them to enjoy what I have given them. If your Heavenly Father has blessed you, do you think he wants you to enjoy some of it in a personal way? Is it a big blessing or a small blessing? We are to love our neighbour as we love ourself, so we are told in many places, for example Mark 12:31. Our Father tells us to love ourselves, and model our neighbour-loving on that.

So, why has your Father blessed you during this season of everything going right? Ask yourself, and ask him. Consider how to extend the kingdom, who needs generosity, and how your Father wants to bless you personally.

Be generous.

Generosity is also important as an antidote to the temptation of selfishness during times of 'everything going right'. One might feel that being generous would be easy when everything is going well financially, but that is not necessarily the case. There are people who always find generosity difficult. I am sure that they have other fine qualities, but we should always be generous. Considering our Heavenly Father's generosity to us is quite helpful. Also, we can be too busy to be generous, as described above.

There can be a temptation to be patronising. In fact, we can be so whilst being oblivious to it. Our attitude to others is the critical factor, and we need to realise that before God we all have the same status. There should never be any suggestion that one is superior because one has more money. Jesus is Lord of all, and *everything* is his, yet he walked amongst us in true humility.

Maintain fellowship.

There are many good reasons for meeting with the people of God, and not just to worship. Obviously our Father desires this, because he tells us not to 'forsake' doing so (Hebrews 10:25). It is important that we identify with the people of God, and work together. I am made in the image of God, and I love to see my family together, and with me. Our Father does too.

But there is another important aspect to fellowship when we are doing well. Mixing with a variety of people, such as there should be in church, and observing their qualities and strengths, is good for us. The rich learn to appreciate those of more modest means, because they receive from them. When I see another person's gifting, and see them blessing others, or me, with it, I really start to appreciate and respect them. During the times when everything is going well, real fellowship with a variety of real people helps keep our feet on the ground.

Accountability.

There have been Christian movements and churches where accountability has been a contentious issue. The 'heavy shepherding' movement, where members had to divulge almost every personal detail of their life to a spiritual line manager, did not work. If a member was being dishonest at work, he would not tell his cell group leader, or elder. Likewise if he was being unfaithful to his wife, or getting involved in other seriously sinful activity. And when the elder ran off with his secretary, people wondered who *he* had been accountable to. There is also the other extreme where people say they are accountable, *only to Jesus*. One asks oneself what they have got to hide, because that is what it sounds like.

But accountability is important. Most of all, I want someone I can trust. I also want someone who really cares about me. A further requirement is that they will observe confidentiality. Personally, I find all these attributes in Wendy, my wife. We trust each other, and can be quite honest with one another. I find that this is accountability that works.

I have been in situations where accountability has not worked, and has left me extremely suspicious concerning speaking of matters of a personal nature to anyone. I was warned against sharing too much information with the leader of one church I was a member of, because 'he does talk rather freely about people's personal lives once he's had a couple of glasses of wine'. In another church, the leader told me things about other members' sex lives that, firstly, he should never have divulged, and secondly, that I just don't believe were true in at least one case. The people concerned were out of favour with the leadership. I was so shocked on one occasion, that I was literally speechless. On another I asked if he should be telling me that.

Accountability works best with true friends. Proverbs 20:6 tells us that the wounds of a friend are faithful. Rod brought me a word from God that was wounding, but necessary (Chapter 3). Another friend said, "Repent, or you'll go to hell". Those men were true friends who cared about me. Within such a relationship of friendship, and within a good marriage, accountability works. Find true friends and invest time and trust.

Pay your taxes.

Many people who have a season of 'everything going right' financially are self-employed. The temptation to cheat the taxman is very strong, because the opportunities are numerous. Accepting cash and not declaring it is rife, if national statistics on the subject are to be believed. But it is not just the taxman who is cheated, but everybody else in the country. Others have to pay more tax, and there is less money for financing health and education, and paying benefits, etc. to those who deserve them. Everybody else pays taxes for those who cheat.

The person who is most affected by cheating with tax is the Christian who does it. It is sin that comes between that person and their God. They can appear spiritually healthy on the outside, but their spiritual state on the inside is a different matter. Additionally, they will not be entrusted with true spiritual riches (Luke 16:11). Maybe the church will trust them spiritually, and maybe the leadership will entrust them with ministry - but it is unlikely that the Lord will, because his word says such a person shall not be trusted in these ways. Don't cheat with your taxes.

Testify.

Finally, when everything is going right for you, glorify Jesus. I like to tell people how the Lord blessed me through my dental practices. I speak of my mediocrity at all things academic - so it was not me being clever. I speak of how I let the Lord down - so he was not rewarding good behaviour. I speak of lessons learned, and of how slow I am to learn, so often. Therefore it has to be the kindness and love of God. Testify. Tell others with words, and show them with action, and impact them with attitude.

* * * * *

There are many dangers and temptations along the way when everything is going right - but the opportunities to extend the kingdom, bless others and testify to the kindness of our Father in heaven, are myriad. Let us resist the devil, seize the opportunities, extend the kingdom, bless others, and glorify Jesus.

* * * * *

The Bible says, *'As for the rich in this present age, charge them not to be haughty, nor to set their hopes on the uncertainty of riches, but on God, who richly provides us with everything to enjoy'. 1 Timothy 6:17.*

'Therefore let him who thinks he stands take heed that he does not fall'. 1 Corinthians 10:12.

Chapter 20

Be Happy!

"My son Terry has just moved in with a new girlfriend. She's got three kids by three different men, and all they do is shout and argue. Terry says she's got terrible debts. He says he goes down the pub for some peace and quiet. But as long as he's happy; that's the main thing, I say. As long as he's happy".

Those words might not be precisely what I heard several years ago when a lady I knew would talk about her son in that manner, but they are close enough. Happy? I would have loved to have known her definition and understanding of the word 'happy'. And I felt sorry for Terry, whose happiness I had really serious doubts about.

* * * * *

'So long as you're happy' and 'whatever makes you happy' are two phrases that betray the fact that so many people feel that happiness is to be sought above all else. The word is often used in a superficial manner, and is usually related to happenings. When good things happen, you are happy. When bad things happen, you are unhappy. So life needs to be a continuous stream of good things. And sometimes it is necessary to pretend, such as when your son moves in with an indebted woman with shouting, arguing children sired by innumerable previous partners.

At least one modern translation of the Bible has the word 'happy' where more traditional versions read 'blessed'. I think some of us would have reservations when it is used in a context such as 'Happy are those who mourn'. Have I been happy during times of mourning? I think not, though I may have been blessed.

The same translation uses happiness again in Acts 20:35, where we read, 'The Lord Jesus himself said, "There is more happiness in giving than in receiving"'. So, does giving make you happy?

* * * * *

Can you remember when you were a child, waiting for Christmas? You might have been different from me, but the days dragged and the few weeks of early December seemed to last forever. I was so excited. What was I going to *get*? The happiness was in *receiving*. It was in both the anticipation and the actual realisation, when I eventually held present after present in my hand. Was I excited about *giving*? Not at all, because I did not give presents to anybody. I was a child, and it was all about receiving.

These days, Christmas is different. I still receive presents, but significantly fewer. With six daughters, four sons-in-law, and nineteen grandchildren, I delegate most of the giving to Wendy. Curiously, she seems to enjoy it, as she considers what each family member would like to receive. I feel no excitement about what I might receive, though I am often pleasantly surprised on the day.

Shopping for a gift for Wendy can be exciting. Why? Because I imagine how she will feel when she opens it. I empathise, and I think we all do at such times. Giving can be much more fun than receiving.

When I was a child, the excitement lay in receiving. Now I am an adult, the joy lies in giving. Such joy is an aspect of maturity, and this is true within the context of Paul's words to the Ephesians elders in Acts 20:35.

I have already said that there is no place in the kingdom of God for meanies. We are called to be like our Father in heaven, and give generously; in fact, to give as a lifestyle. Giving in time, to those in the family, to those in the family of God, and strangers. Giving time, giving attention, *listening* to people, giving friendship, and giving money. And if we give as God gives, and as Jesus taught, we will be *blessed*.

* * * * *

I do not have illusions about happiness, and nor do I chase after it. Good things happen, and make me happy, but a more realistic goal is joy. Another is fulfilment. We may not deserve either, but our Heavenly Father delights to favour his children with both. We are blessed indeed.

Do you want to be blessed in a world that dishes out disappointment daily? Do you want fulfilment in a society where people strive for elusive happiness, and yet remain unfulfilled and dissatisfied? You will find what you seek only in relationship with our God, and through the person of Jesus. And a person in that relationship is someone who gives.

I have been a member of the Full Gospel Businessmen (FGB) for a few decades now. The story of how this global fellowship of men was called into being by God, through the ministry of Demos Shakarian in the mid-twentieth century, is told in the book, *The Happiest People on Earth*. But you do not need to join the FGB in order to experience happiness, though many good things happen during our meetings (and in everyday life) that bring much happiness. We see peoples' lives changed, as the sick get healed, addicts are set free, marriages restored, and so on. However, happiness (often) with fulfilment and joy (continuous) are on offer to whosoever.

Not all Christians are happy, but those who give are nearly always happy. And blessed. Mean people are often hard pressed financially, or 'hard up' as we say in the UK. That's because they do not give, and Jesus said, "Give, and it shall be given to *you*" (Luke 6:38). Jesus did not make mistakes - we need to be those who give. Christians who do not give are not greatly blessed. Jesus said that we are more blessed when we give than when we receive (Acts 20:35). Are you blessed when you receive? Of course you are, but you are *more* blessed when you give. So give.

If happiness is one of your goals in life, and it is a legitimate one, have a proper relationship with Jesus - and give generously. If you want your children and grandchildren to know real happiness in life, rôle model and demonstrate a real relationship with your Heavenly Father, and be like him - be generous. You will be blessed indeed, and will have happiness and joy of a quality unknown to those of the world.

If you handle your finances in a godly manner, you will be entrusted with true riches (Luke 16:11). You will be a blessing in your marriage and your family, your church and your community. You will be a kingdom builder. You will please the Father as you walk in the Spirit and honour the Son. To be such a person is to walk in the blessing of God that 'makes rich and brings no sorrow', (Proverbs 10:22). Be such a person.

* * * * *

The Bible says, *'There is more happiness in giving than in receiving'. Acts 20:35.*

Chapter 21

Promises, Promises!

The following Bible verses are in three sections. The first section is verses that tell us the nature of our Heavenly Father. It is true that there are many different facets and aspects to the character of God, and that he is a God of anger, for instance, as well as a God of love. The verses in section one are those that speak of the sort of *Father* he is to his children. Read these verses and meditate on them. Allow the Spirit to take them and speak them into your heart. Faith comes by hearing – so listen. The purpose of this is for you to have real faith concerning your Heavenly Father. (If you have never come to a place where you have truly put your trust in the Lord, and know what it is to be born again into a whole new life, then you need to do so. Maybe contact me through my website – the web address is on the back cover – or contact your nearest chapter of the Full Gospel Businessmen, or a local evangelical or Pentecostal church). When you have real faith concerning who your Heavenly Father really is, you will find it is almost automatic to trust him to give you good gifts, success, prosperity, health, and the other things he has promised.

The second section is *promises* that the Lord has made in the Bible. They are for *YOU!* So read them and meditate on them, and allow the Holy Spirit to speak them to you, so that you have concrete faith in them. Have the type of faith we read of in Hebrews 11, and which is defined in verse 1. Have the type of faith that pleases God (Hebrews 11:6).

Finally, there is a third section that speaks of the sort of people we will be if we really believe the truth found in sections two and three. This is because we have a responsibility to live lives that please our Father, and if we really believe he is a loving Father, and if we really believe that he has made us wonderful promises and follows through to give us a wonderful life, then this is *how* we shall live. There is teaching today that has been labeled 'extreme grace' teaching. It rightly emphasises the grace of God towards us, but is very light on our responsibility to live lives pleasing to him. The result has been, in many instances, that sexual immorality and other ungodly living, is virtually excused by saying that 'we are under grace'. Such Christians live their lives in a manner that is no different from people with worldly values and culture. *We are called to be different.* I will not elaborate, as the scriptures I am placing in section three make it abundantly clear that we are on this earth to please God. Let us never take the grace and lovingkindness of our Father for granted, and act presumptuously in a sinful manner.

So, get faith! Be full of faith in a God whose heart is for his children to prosper and be in good health, even as their soul prospers. (2 John 3).

Bible verses that tell us about the nature of our Heavenly Father.

'Father of the fatherless and protector of widows is God in his holy habitation'. Psalm 68:5.

'As a father shows compassion to his children, so the LORD shows compassion to those who fear him'. Psalm 103:13.

'For to us a child is born, to us a son is given; and the government shall be upon his shoulder, and his name shall be called Wonderful Counselor, Mighty God, Everlasting Father, Prince of Peace'. Isaiah 9:6.

'For God so loved the world, that he gave his only Son, that whoever believes in him should not perish but have eternal life'. John 3:16.

'Blessed be the God and Father of our Lord Jesus Christ, the Father of mercies and God of all comfort, who comforts us in all our affliction, so that we may be able to comfort those who are in any affliction, with the comfort with which we ourselves are comforted by God'. 2 Corinthians 1:3-4.

'Grace to you and peace from God our Father and the Lord Jesus Christ'. Galatians 1:3.

'Blessed be the God and Father of our Lord Jesus Christ, who has blessed us in Christ with every spiritual blessing in the heavenly places'. Ephesians 1:3.

'Every good gift and every perfect gift is from above, coming down from the Father of lights with whom there is no variation or shadow due to change'. James 1:17.

'See what kind of love the Father has given to us, that we should be called children of God; and so we are'. 1 John 3:1.

If you meditate on just one of these verses, this is the one –

***'For God so loved the world, that he gave his only Son, that whoever believes in him should not perish but have eternal life'*. John 3:16.**

Bible verses that are promises to us from the Lord.

1. *'And if you faithfully obey the voice of the Lord your God, being careful to do all his commandments that I command you today, the Lord your God will set you high above all the nations of the earth.*

2 *And all these blessings shall come upon you and overtake you, if you obey the voice of the Lord your God.*

3 *Blessed shall you be in the city, and blessed shall you be in the field.*

4 *Blessed shall be the fruit of your womb and the fruit of your ground and the fruit of your cattle, the increase of your herds and the young of your flock.*

5 *Blessed shall be your basket and your kneading bowl.*

6 *Blessed shall you be when you come in, and blessed shall you be when you go out.*

7 *The Lord will cause your enemies who rise against you to be defeated before you. They shall come out against you one way and flee before you seven ways.*

8 *The Lord will command the blessing on you in your barns and in all that you undertake. And he will bless you in the land that the Lord your God is giving you.*

9 *The Lord will establish you as a people holy to himself, as he has sworn to you, if you keep the commandments of the Lord your God and walk in his ways.*

10 *And all the peoples of the earth shall see that you are called by the name of the Lord, and they shall be afraid of you.*

11 *And the Lord will make you abound in prosperity, in the fruit of your womb and in the fruit of your livestock and in the fruit of your ground, within the land that the Lord swore to your fathers to give you.*

12 *The Lord will open to you his good treasury, the heavens, to give the rain to your land in its season and to bless all the work of your hands. And you shall lend to many nations, but you shall not borrow.*

13 *And the Lord will make you the head and not the tail, and you shall only go up and not down, if you obey the commandments of the Lord your God, which I command you today, being careful to do them,*

14 *and if you do not turn aside from any of the words that I command you today, to the right hand or to the left, to go after other gods to serve them'.* Deuteronomy 28:1-14.

'*This book of the law shall not depart from your mouth, but you shall meditate on it day and night, so that you may be careful to do according to all that is written in it; for then you will make your way prosperous, and then you will have success*'. Joshua 1:8.

'*Honour the LORD with your wealth and with the firstfruits of all your produce; then your barns will be filled with plenty, and your vats will be bursting with wine*'. Proverbs 3:9-10.

'*Blessed is the man who walks not in the counsel of the wicked, nor stands in the way of sinners, nor sits in the seat of scoffers; but his delight is in the law of the LORD, and on his law he meditates day and night. He is like a tree planted by streams of water that yields its fruit in its season, and its leaf does not wither. In all that he does, he prospers*'. Psalm 1:1-3

'*Let those who delight in my righteousness shout for joy and be glad and say evermore, 'Great is the LORD, who delights in the welfare of his servant!*' Psalm 35:27

'Delight yourself in the LORD, and He will give you the desires of your heart'. Psalm 37:4

'One gives freely, yet grows all the richer; another withholds what he should give, and only suffers want. Whoever brings blessing will be enriched, and one who waters will himself be watered'. Proverbs 11:24,25.

'The blessing of the LORD makes rich, and he adds no sorrow with it'. Proverbs 10:22.

'The reward for humility and fear of the LORD is riches and honor and life'. Proverbs 22:4.

'Whoever has a bountiful eye will be blessed, for he shares his bread with the poor'. Proverbs 22:9.

'Whoever gives to the poor will not want, but he who hides his eyes will get many a curse'. Proverbs 28:27.

'But when you give to the needy, do not let your left hand know what your right hand is doing, so that your giving may be in secret. And your Father who sees in secret will reward you'. Matthew 6:3-4.

'Give, and it will be given to you. Good measure, pressed down, shaken together, running over, will be put into your lap. For with the measure you use it will be measured back to you'. Luke 6:38.

'If you then, who are evil, know how to give good gifts to your children, how much more will the heavenly Father give the Holy Spirit to those who ask'. Luke 11:13.

'The point is this: whoever sows sparingly will also reap sparingly, and whoever sows bountifully will also reap bountifully. Each one must give as he has decided in his heart, not reluctantly or under compulsion, for God loves a cheerful giver. And God is able to make all grace abound to you, so that having all sufficiency in all things at all times, you may abound in every good work'. 2 Corinthians 9:6-8.

'Beloved, I pray that you may prosper in all things and be in health, just as your soul prospers'. 3 John 2.

The following is a description of how the Lord blessed Joseph, a faithful man of God, when he arrived in Egypt.

'The LORD was with Joseph so that he prospered, and he lived in the house of his Egyptian master. When his master saw that the LORD was with him and that the LORD gave him success in everything he did, Joseph found favor in his eyes and became his attendant. Potiphar put him in charge of his household, and he entrusted to his care everything he owned. From the time he put him in charge of his household and of all that he owned, the LORD blessed the household of the Egyptian because of Joseph. The blessing of the LORD was on everything Potiphar had, both in the house and in the field. So Potiphar left everything he had in Joseph's care; with Joseph in charge, he did not concern himself with anything except the food he ate. Now Joseph was well-built and handsome'. Genesis 39:2-6.

If you meditate on just one of these verses, this is the one –

'Beloved, I pray that you may prosper in all things and be in health, just as your soul prospers'. 3 John 2.

Responsibilities, Responsibilities.

Bible verses that instruct us in how to live.

'Therefore everyone who hears these words of Mine and acts on them, may be compared to a wise man who built his house on the rock. And the rain fell, and the floods came, and the winds blew and slammed against that house; and yet it did not fall, for it had been founded on the rock'. Matthew 7:24,25.

'If you love Me, you will keep My commandments'. John 14:15.

'Do not be conformed to this world, but be transformed by the renewal of your mind, that by testing you may discern what is the will of God, what is good and acceptable and perfect'. Romans 12:1.

'But the fruit of the Spirit is love, joy, peace, patience, kindness, goodness, faithfulness, gentleness, self-control; against such things there is no law'. Galatians 5:22,23.

'But be doers of the word, and not hearers only, deceiving yourselves'. James 1:22.

'What use is it, my brethren, if someone says he has faith but he has no works? Can that faith save him? If a brother or sister is without clothing and in need of daily food, and one of you says to them, "Go in peace, be warmed and be filled", and yet you do not give them what is necessary for their body, what use is that?' James 2:14-16.

If you meditate on just one of these verses, this is the one –

***'Do not be conformed to this world, but be transformed by the renewal of your mind, that by testing you may discern what is the will of God, what is good and acceptable and perfect'.* Romans 12:1.**

I Am Indebted...

We are instructed not to be in debt to anyone, except that we should love them (Romans 13:8). I am indebted to many people for their positive input into my life over many years; here, I would like to thank the few who have helped me understand money, especially the Biblical principles involved.

The Bible is a wonderful source of all wisdom, including financial, and is in a league of its own with regard to the impartation of truth. With the Holy Spirit to interpret and give life to its words, one needs nothing else. In fact, I have found no other book that comes anywhere near the word of God with regard to teaching us the truth. Prosperity teaching books are encouraging and faith building, but can be somewhat detached from the real world where things go wrong, and where budgeting is necessary.

Secular books can be helpful - or not. I saw a book that purported to show the reader how to become a multimillionaire quickly. I knew someone who would enjoy it, and so bought a copy. Perhaps it would help me too? I read the Introduction, only to be informed that if I was over forty, then it was already too late. I was around sixty!

My parents taught me the value of money, by their attitude towards it. They did not have too much, my father worked hard for what they had, and both were careful with it. They encouraged me to study until I was twenty-five, receiving virtually nothing, but expecting to have a slightly higher income later by way of reward. I am grateful to them for their example and encouragement. Otherwise, as already stated, it has been the Bible and the Holy Spirit.

Barry Harvey has again been invaluable in proofreading, as has my wife Wendy. Don Double and his PA, Gill Hunkin, read through the manuscript prior to publication, and I am indebted to them for their critical appraisal and corrections of typos. Derek Blois has excelled with the cover design. Derek has become something of a celebrity artist in recent years, and deservedly so. His work can be viewed at the *PictureCraft Gallery & Exhibition Centre*, in Holt, Norfolk, and online at *www.picturecraftgallery.co.uk/derek-blois-bahons-aiea/*

Daughters encourage me in all things good. A number of grandchildren have requested, and received, signed copies of previous books. What a lovely statement that made.

My wife Wendy is not only the very epitome of patience as I sit and tap away at my iPad, or vanish into my study to edit on the desktop; she actually encourages me, as she knows the sense of fulfilment I gain from writing. What a truly lovely lady she is. I thank my Heavenly Father daily for blessing me with such a helpmeet, partner, lover and friend.

Most of all, I thank the Lord Jesus, who changed my life for ever in October 1965, and who gives me foretastes of heaven now, with so much more to come. As we read in 2 Corinthians 8:9, though He was rich, He became poor, in order that we might become rich. Amen!

THERE MUST BE MORE TO LIFE THAN THIS!
How to know the God of the Bible in Everyday Life

by Barrie Lawrence

Published by New Wine Press (2012)

Barrie writes in his own distinctive style of incidents in his life that can only be described as amazing coincidences – or acts of God!

Barrie sent a paperback book to a patient, as he thought it would be helpful. The patient's wife took it from the postman, panicked, and called the emergency services to say a bomb had just been delivered. Why? A lady Barrie had known several years earlier, was woken up in the night to hear the Lord say to her, "Pray for Barrie Lawrence." Years later she was amazed to find out just why! And there was the time when a teapot prevented Barrie from really enjoying life as it was meant to be. How could that be? And then again there was the time when he and his wife were called to a school to heal a boy with a deformed arm – and the whole class were waiting to watch the miracle.

Not without humour, Barrie writes of the ways *he* has been challenged on various occasions in his life, of his successes and his failures. It's OK to laugh at him at times, because he does so himself, but you may also want to weep with him as he opens his heart about coping with difficulties and heartbreaks. Above all, it is an inspiring book that seeks to lift the reader onto a higher plane in life.

The first half of the book, part one, comprises fifteen short chapters of true stories from Barrie's own life, while part two has a clear message – it's happened to me and it can happen to you. In fact, part two is a reader-friendly guide to help anyone to come to know the God who we read about in the Bible.

If there are times when you think to yourself, "There must be more to life than this", then this book is a *must-read* for you!

Available from www.amazon.co.uk and all good bookshops.

A brilliant book by Barrie Lawrence. For anyone asking, **'Is there more to life than this?'** the author reveals a resounding 'Yes'. He shares his own journey of faith with refreshing candour – and then shows how the reader can experience Life with a capital L.

Michael Wiltshire, *author and journalist, and a director of FGB, the world's largest fellowship for Christian businessmen.*

Barrie Lawrence writes for Christians who compare their uneventful lives to all the excitement they read about in the Bible, and want to experience more of the latter. He shares some of his life story from nearly 50 years of being a Christian before pointing his readers to pointers for experiencing God for themselves. A sincere and candid little book.

Christianity Magazine, *April 2013*

Barrie has an infectious enthusiasm about the things of God and a burning desire to share them with others. The underlying theme is the breaking in of the supernatural to ordinary lives, and the importance of experiencing as well as believing.

Network Norwich, *February 2013*

THE CURIOUS CASE OF THE CONSTIPATED CAT – and Other True Stories of Answered Prayer

by Barrie Lawrence

Published by Grosvenor House (2016)

A terminally constipated pussy cat, two frozen shoulders, a man with a broken arm, a boy with a deformed arm, broken relationships, work overload, lost at night in a foreign city, irritable bowel, Crohn's Disease, financial challenges, wanting a husband, wanting a wife, not wanting divorce... All these needs were met after prayer. Coincidences? Psychosomatic? Don't be so silly. Come on - get real! Barrie and Wendy Lawrence, two very ordinary people, say, "If He can do it for us, then He can do it for you". Is anything too hard for the LORD? Get a realistic, meaningful relationship with the King of kings, and be amazed at what He can do in *your* life. This book is all about JESUS!

Available from www.amazon.co.uk in the United Kingdom, and www.amazon.com in North America, and from all good bookshops

* * *

"Feel your faith rise as you read these stories of answered prayer - faith to reach out to the God who can meet *your* need too".

Don Double, Evangelist and Founder, Good News Crusade.

"It's not the most conventional title for a Christian book. But then Barrie Lawrence is no average author. *The Curious Case of the Constipated Cat and Other True Stories of Answered*

Prayer is the fourth book penned by Mr. Lawrence, a dentist, author and speaker. The book is different because not many 'religious books' are written in (his) style. Well, look at the title for a start! It is a collection of true stories of answered prayer, ranging from a cat being cured of constipation, and fog suddenly lifting so a flight could take off, to a troubled marriage being saved".

Eastern Daily Press *Review by Ian Clarke, 26th March 2016*

Good storytellers attract and engage their audiences quickly. Barrie, known for his straightforward, compelling and non-jargon style – refreshing for many Christians - has compiled interesting and often entertaining stories of a constipated cat, a boy with a deformed arm, an angel in Venice, a romance restored, an irritable bowel and many more relating to answered prayer. He playfully ends some accounts with a view that some people would consider the outcomes as "it's a coincidence, or maybe psychosomatic".

Enthusiasm underpins Barrie's approach to life. To find out more about the cat and as a helpful guide to answered prayer, do buy the book.

Network Norwich. *Review by Kevin Gotts*

I've just finished a great little book on prayer which I would heartily recommend. *The Curious Case of the Constipated Cat – and Other True Stories of Answered Prayer* was just the easy encouraging read I needed. In his light-hearted way, Barrie recounts various accounts of answered prayer before explaining our relationship with our Heavenly Father, and how we communicate with Him. Using the outline of the Lord's Prayer, Barrie highlights some basics about our relationship with our Heavenly Father and appropriate attitudes to develop an effective prayer life. Some great gems and interesting illustrations on how to approach some of the complexities of faith.

Editorial* in *Three-in-One *magazine of the Christian Dental Fellowship, by Victoria Rushton, President. Summer 2016*

CURIOUS PEOPLE, HUMOROUS HAPPENINGS, CROWNS OF GLORY

A DENTIST'S STORY

by Barrie Lawrence

Published by Grosvenor House Publishing (2014)

After-dinner speaker Barrie Lawrence has been making people laugh - *really* laugh - for years. Now it's your turn to hear his unbelievably funny, sometimes poignant stories from dental school, surgery and life. How did a pet frog lead to a successful career of seven dental surgeries and a bookshop? And of course, he was a student during those years known as the 'Swinging Sixties!'

How can a filling take five hours to complete, and why did one of the lecturers at his dental school describe Barrie qualifying as 'like letting a monkey loose with a pistol'?

Read of some of those incidents and memories that have been making people smile for years when Barrie has been engaged in after-dinner speaking – or simply to the local Women's Institute. Do families of five really share just one toothbrush between them? Do that many dentures sail away down the toilet every winter? Have you ever come across people who share a set of false teeth between them?

But something happened while Barrie was training at the London Hospital – something that was even more important than training as a dentist!

You'll laugh, you'll cry, and most important of all, you will be inspired.

Available from www.amazon.co.uk in the United Kingdom, and www.amazon.com in North America, and from all good bookshops

* * *

"A refreshing delight. The author succeeds in maintaining interest by careful selection of anecdotes combined with a light-hearted tone and appropriate pace. I would recommend this book to anybody… looking for something uncomplicated and entertaining".

British Dental Journal, *Review by T. Doshi, December 2014*

"An entertaining and encouraging read". **Network Norwich.**

PATIENTS FROM HEAVEN – and Other Places!

By Barrie Lawrence

Published by Grosvenor House (2015)

Baron Goldfinger seemed to have stepped straight off the James Bond movie set, Tad the Pole caused the nurses to swoon, while Misty, the flirtatious American lady, suddenly vanished – probably murdered, said the police. These and dozens of other colourful characters walk across the pages of *Patients From Heaven – and Other Places!* During nearly forty years of practice in dental surgery, a wealth of fascinating personalities passed through his surgery. Some were from heaven - and some were from other places! Laugh, smile, gasp, cry, and simply be inspired as you read through these engaging stories from real life.

Available from www.amazon.co.uk (UK), www.amazon.com (North America) and all good bookshops.

* * *

"Barrie introduces us to some of the most memorable people he met in this lovely and engaging memoir, the follow-up of his well-received *A Dentist's Story*. This is a lively read – he has a real way with a tale that keeps you turning the pages. Barrie is a practising Christian, but he doesn't hit you over the head with it; only mentioning it 'as and when' to put his story into context. An enjoyable – and rather uplifting – read".

Eastern Daily Press, *Review by Trevor Heaton, June 2015*

The style of writing reflects Barrie's skill as an engaging and very humorous after dinner speaker. He starts with those (patients) that became friends, or had something that endeared them to him and his staff; others made them laugh, or simply left them feeling better.

How does he depict patients from the *Other Place?* His belief as a born-again Christian, he says, changed everything including the way he sees other people. Courteously, he also sees this category of people with emotions, maybe struggling with relationships or finance. Chapters like "Blue Murder, a Pink Ear, Bubbles and a Bad Smell", "Nice and Nasty" and "The Gift of the Gab" have to be read.

Barrie balances his stories with patient's perceptions about him, with one patient calling him "a dangerous man".

His previous title *"A Dentist's Story"* concluded with an appendix of dental jokes and this time there is an appendix of anecdotes concerning encounters with members of the police force. Chapters including "The Man in Black", "Idiot!", "The Insurance Fraud?" and "A Carnivorous Villain" leave the reader entertained and bursting with laughter.

This book can easily be read and savoured like a meal with many courses over a period or devoured in one long sitting. Ideal as a holiday read and to pass on.

Network Norwich*, Review by Kevin Gotts, August 2015*

Patients from Heaven brilliantly explores Barrie Lawrence's plethora of patient experiences and stories in an equally hilarious and tasteful manner. Being a dental professional exposes us to a vast array of patients providing a wide range of wonderful and not so wonderful memories. Barrie takes us on a journey through all the memorable patients he has seen and all the lessons he has learned, whilst also respecting patient confidentiality (and brilliantly using fictional names and clever puns). *Patients from heaven* is a delightful read.

British Dental Journal, December 2015, Issue 11. *Reviewed by K. Mahmood*

LICENSED TO DRILL – Dentist on the Loose!

By Barrie Lawrence

Published by Grosvenor House (2015)

Licensed to drill! Shots, Killing, Out Cold, Asphyxiated, Agents, Accomplices, Cocaine, the Opposition, The Man with the Golden Tooth, Heroes, Villains and a trip to Russia in the days of the old Soviet Union all figure in this fascinating catalogue of stories from nearly 40 years of being LICENSED TO DRILL!

See just what really goes on at times behind the doors of a dental practice. Three patients fled, one with the dentist in hot pursuit. Fruit pastilles were laced with anaesthetic, and on one occasion, a 'dangerous mongoose' escaped from its cage in the car park. And so much more.

Barrie takes the lid off life in a dental practice in a way that is engaging, entertaining, and totally unforgettable.

Available from www.amazon.co.uk (UK), www.amazon.com (North America) and all good bookshops.

* * *

Former Norfolk dentist Dr. Lawrence delves into 40 years of stories to come up with his third collection of anecdotes. When it comes to the dentist's chair, all human life is there, and Barrie has met many, many kinds of people over the years; the man who insisted on having a gold filling as an investment (it wasn't) to one who was convinced – like that famous Tommy Cooper gag come to life – that his 'teeth itched' (they didn't). As with all of Barrie's books, this is lively, chatty stuff and a very easy (and rather informative) read.

Eastern Daily Press. *Review by Trevor Heaton, May 2017*

The well-known Norfolk author, blogger and storyteller Dr Barrie Lawrence is taking readers on a James Bond-fuelled journey in his new title *LICENSED TO DRILL* Dentist on the Loose!

Barrie almost seems to take on a Bond persona after qualifying, following the facetious remark from his senior registrar, "Lawrence has qualified. That's like letting a monkey loose with a pistol." Soon he was sounding suave and lethal, "It's 006, licensed to drill", aided by the last three digits of his credit card reading 006 and attracting comments, "Going off on any adventures? Yes; this very afternoon. Goldentooth". Strikingly he is a Bond aficionado and has followed and travelled to many of the films' locations.

This is book number five, and the third which is light, dental anecdotal. Besides humour, he delves deeper into the history of, and the everyday workings of dentistry, to reinforce his stories of Heroes, Villains and Memorable Others - all written in his engaging and entertaining style.

This book will be loved by his growing following of loyal readers. And for those new to Barrie's writings, go and treat yourself to a fill of entertaining and amusing stories from behind the dental practice doors.

Network Norwich. Review from Kevin Gotts, June 2017

Cleverly playing on the credentials of the legendary British spy, Barrie has weaved an adventure with anecdotes and intrigue from stories across some 40 years' service as a dental surgeon.

The movie Goldeneye helped ignite requests from customers looking to use gold as a material for restoring teeth, and for others to display a glint of gold. Barrie decided to visit the old Soviet Union to see the excesses of upper front teeth crowned with gold and recalls being "followed by our faithful FGB tail – so I kept my mouth well and truly shut", Barrie confesses.

Barrie has a strong moral compass, reinforced by his Christian faith, and like Bond is hospitable to all he comes across. This book will be loved by his growing following of loyal readers.

Good News for Norwich. Review by Kevin Gotts, December 2017

Although not every dental professional may choose to read dental themed literature for pleasure, some amusement may be found in this text. A light-hearted read, Barrie Lawrence's latest book presents a series of well-intentioned dental anecdotes from a long career in the profession.

The author is open from the outset regarding his spiritual beliefs and the resultant impact on his writing – the consequence, specified by the author himself, is an inoffensive text, free of any crude or inappropriate content. On this basis, it is a very accessible book for those wanting to hear about the reality of working with the general public in a challenging profession.

In summary, though this may not be the author's intention, the book may be suited to a younger individual considering a career in dentistry as the stories provide some basic history of dentistry and a real insight into the characters faced in daily practice with sprinklings of basic dental science education thrown in.

British Dental Journal Volume 224 Issue 476 13th April 2018 Review by Andrew Geddis-Regan